The Encyclopedia of Angels
Spirit Guides & Ascended Masters

A Guide to 200 Celestial Beings
to Help, Heal, and Assist You in Everyday Life

Susan Gregg

FAIR WINDS
PRESS
BEVERLY, MASSACHUSETTS

Dedication
I'd like to dedicate this book to the place within each person
that longs to connect with their divinity and is willing to take
the often arduous journey to make that connection possible.

Text © 2008 Fair Winds Press

First published in the USA in 2008 by
Fair Winds Press, a member of
Quayside Publishing Group
100 Cummings Center
Suite 406-L
Beverly, Massachusetts 01915-6101
Telephone: 978.282.9590
Fax: 978.283.2742
www.fairwindspress.com

12 11 10 09   3 4 5

ISBN-13: 978-1-59233-343-1
ISBN-10: 1-59233-343-5

Library of Congress Cataloging-in-Publication Data
Gregg, Susan 1949–
      The encyclopedia of angels, spirit guides, and ascended masters : a guide to
   200 celestial beings to help, heal, and assist you in everyday life / Susan Gregg.
        p.   cm.
      ISBN-13: 978-1-59233-343-1
      ISBN-10: 1-59233-343-5
      1. Angels—Encyclopedias. 2. Guides (Spiritualism)—Encyclopedias.
   3. Ascended masters—Encyclopedias. I. Title
   BL477.G75 2008
   202'.1—dc22   2007044632

Cover design: doublemranch.com
Book design: John Barnett
Book production: Colleen Cunningham
Illustrations: Wendy Edelson

Printed and bound in China

Contents

Introduction

This encyclopedia is just a tiny glimpse into the world of angels, saints, ascended masters, gods, goddesses, and deities. There are literally thousands of spiritual icons. Availing yourself of their wisdom and knowledge can be a fun and exciting process. Getting to know them is certainly enjoyable and enlightening. Working with them on a regular basis can vastly improve the quality of your life and facilitate your spiritual explorations.

I am so grateful I was asked to write this book. I began my own spiritual explorations as a young girl. I always had a curiosity about life and what, if anything, existed beyond the perception of my physical senses. Originally I wanted to be a nuclear physicist and explore the subatomic world. Quantum physics has shown me I have explored the same territory. I just arrived there from a different direction.

I never really knew much about saints, but as I researched their lives, I found them fascinating. At first I was struck by the pain and suffering they experienced in their lives, but then I noticed the theme of peace and acceptance. Even when they were being tortured to death, witnesses reported an incredible sense of peace emanating from them. These people dedicated their lives to developing and deepening their connection with God and, in the process, developed the ability to perform miracles. Many of the saints were able to do amazing things. They were able to levitate, bilocate, and turn water into wine. These men and women taught me a lot.

I pored over thousands of names, not only of saints, but also of angels, ascended masters, gods, goddesses, and deities, deciding whom to include in this book. Their lives inspired me to trust the process. I opened up my mind and my heart, and this book was born. It seemed to take on a life of its own. At times it felt like it was unfolding before my eyes.

Give yourself the gift of getting to know them. I have found it helpful to approach the beings in this book with curiosity. Time and again, just when I thought I knew all about an angel or saint or deity, I would be surprised by another facet of their personality. After numerous surprises I began to approach the whole process with an open mind and a great deal of curiosity.

As I continued to work with this wide assortment of angels, saints, ascended masters, gods, goddesses, and deities, I began to imagine a huge school bus. At each stop a variety of individuals would get on and off. The more spiritual icons I let on the bus, the more knowledge there was available to me. No matter how many got on or off, I was still driving the bus, but I had their wisdom and knowledge available to me. I could ask them for directions or for their assistance. As I continued to work on this book, I realized their love and wisdom was always available to me—all I had to do was ask.

Now these beings have become part of my everyday life. Sometimes it feels like the bus is already pretty full, but there always seems to be room for one more. The variety of perspectives and the different world views each of these beings brings with them is very expansive. The world view of an Aborigine living in Australia is certainly very different from a woman growing up in Ireland two thousand years ago. Yet, their feelings and views about life are still alive in Blodeuwedd and in the Wandjina.

As you get to know the beings in this book, your world view will expand and your ability to connect with other people will deepen.

You hold in your hands a book filled with love, wisdom, and immense possibilities. Make these angels, saints, ascended masters, gods, goddesses, and deities your friends. Talk to them, ask for their help, allow them to join you as you journey through your life, moving toward greater freedom, joy, and love. They are certainly more than willing to help you. As soon as you ask and are willing to accept their aid, they will be there. They always respect your free will. They will never impose themselves on you.

Just as a trip around the world changes a person, your life can be transformed by working with these beings from all over the globe. You really can get to know them. Imagine they are your new neighbors. Spend time with them, talk to them, ask them questions, and see what happens.

Working with these beings is one of many steps you can take toward a rich and satisfying spiritual life. The angels, saints, ascended masters, gods, goddesses, and deities in this book are only a small fraction of those that are available to you. They represent a cross section. They are an introduction to the fascinating world of spiritual teachers and guides. There isn't even a need to believe in a particular god or angel in order to work with that god or angel. Spirituality isn't about beliefs; it is about having a direct experience. Play with these entities long enough, and I can guarantee you will have lots of experiences! I was amazed at the incredible presence each of these beings has. Writing this book was like going to a party and interviewing a lot of intriguing people. You now have the opportunity to read those interviews. Read this book with curiosity and an open mind. Thumb through the pages and see who catches your attention. If a certain god or goddess resonates with you, explore that particular tradition in greater depth. As I wrote about the Hindu deities, I was fascinated by them. I love the idea of endless beginnings and endings. Their gods are all so colorful and alive. The stories of their lives are used to teach children morals and lessons about life and to show people how to experience happiness, freedom, and joy.

I have had the honor to study with several indigenous teachers. Their love, wisdom, and guidance have totally transformed my life. As I wrote about some of the deities from those traditions, my understanding of their culture and their world view has deepened. I hope you will allow yourself to be touched by these amazing beings. Open your heart and mind to them. Allow yourself the time to get to know them.

How to Use This Book

How do you get to know angels, saints, ascended masters, gods, goddesses, and deities? It is really very simple; it just isn't necessarily easy. I wasn't taught as a child how to quiet my mind and listen to the angels speaking to me. As a matter of fact, as a young girl, I was discouraged from talking to my imaginary playmate.

There are many ways you can work with this book. It is beautiful, so you can just have it as a coffee-table book. Simply leave it sitting out somewhere where you can see it. When you feel compelled, browse through it at your leisure. No doubt you'll be inspired by what you read.

Alternately, if you have a specific concern, you can look in the index and find several potential helpers. Suppose, for example, that you've lost your keys. By turning to the index, you'll discover that Saint Anthony is a whiz at finding lost objects, so you can say a little prayer asking him to help you and then go happily about your life because you found your keys. The same is true when you need help with larger concerns, such as mending a broken relationship or conceiving a child.

What I hope you'll do, though, is to read through the book and use it on a regular basis. Read about each of the entities and, when you have a specific problem, ask the one you feel the most comfortable with to help you. The more you use this book, the more benefits you will receive. These beings are literally just waiting for you to give them permission to help you, so ask for their help and open your heart and your mind to receive their wonderful guidance. The more familiar you become with them, the easier it will be to know whom to call on.

I can tell you from personal experience that if you really want to change your life, spend some time getting to know the angels, saints, and deities. Work with them on a regular basis. I have been meditating for more than thirty years and have been teaching people about personal growth, meditation, and spirituality for almost two decades. The process of writing this book and actually working with these beings has changed my life immensely. In a very short time, the way I feel, how I see life, and my responses to life have changed a lot. My world has taken on a totally new dimension. I always assumed saints were all about suffering and martyrdom, but as I researched, I found their lives were actually wonderful examples of the peace, joy, and magic a profound connection to the divine can bring. As I read about all the incredible things they were able to do simply by meditating and praying on a regular basis, I realized I could do that as well. Knowing about their lives brought new meaning to my personal meditation time. If they can overcome huge obstacles, just think about what you can do with their assistance! The same gifts are waiting for you.

Begin by spending a few minutes each day tuning in. Meditation is such an easy process, yet we can make it so complicated and downright hard. The easiest way to meditate is to follow your breath. Just notice your breathing. Your mind will think; that's what it does. To successfully meditate, let your mind think but keep bringing your attention back to your breath.

When I teach people how to meditate, I suggest they imagine they are standing on a platform in a train station. Lots of trains come and go. You can get on them and go for a ride, or stand on the platform and watch them go by. If you do get on a train, you can easily get off at the next station. Meditating is a process of standing on the platform and watching your thoughts go by. If you find yourself lost in thought, notice and bring your attention back to your breath. You may have to do that a lot at first, and that is part of the process. As with anything in life, allow yourself to enjoy the process.

The saints meditated and prayed for hours a day. I doubt you have that much time, but I am sure you could set aside fifteen or twenty minutes each day. Spiritual practices do take practice, so allow yourself to practice quieting your mind and allow it to be easy and enjoyable. If you avoid judging the process, you can actually enjoy learning to meditate. After you have focused your attention on your breath for a few minutes, ask one of the saints or angels or deities to work with you, and then allow yourself to feel their presence. I can guarantee you they will be there as soon as you call on them, but it may take you some time to feel their presence or hear their guidance. With a bit of practice, you will be amazed at how comforting and empowering it can be to work with these beings.

Be gentle and loving with yourself as you begin to open up to their presence. At any given moment, your mind is filtering out literally hundreds of pieces of information. If it didn't, you would be so overwhelmed by all the input you wouldn't be able to function. For a moment focus your attention on your sense of sound. Listen to all of the noises in your world that you weren't even con-scious of. Listen for the wind outside and the sounds of your house or your neighborhood. Listen carefully until you can hear your own heartbeat. Once you focus your attention on your hearing, it is amazing what you unconsciously tune out.

As you begin to focus your attention on the angels, saints, ascended masters, gods, goddesses, and deities, you'll find the same thing happening. Those entities have always been there, just at the edge of your reality, waiting for you to invite them into your life. Listen for their gentle whispers. Take the time to patiently listen.

You can create a ceremony or ritual to get in touch with them. A ceremony or ritual is a sacred act. It is something you do mindfully and with a specific purpose in mind. It can be complex or very simple. You can light a candle, say a prayer, or create a sacred space in your home dedicated to honoring the angels, saints, and deities. Decide what feels right to you and go with it. What might feel appropriate one day may not the next day, so remain open and flexible. Follow your heart and listen to your inner wisdom.

Let the gods guide you. Open the book randomly and see who wants to work with you today. Above all, allow yourself to enjoy the process. I had a t-shirt that said, "Angels fly because they take themselves lightly." May the beings in this book help you take yourself lightly, fly high, and enjoy your life.

May you feel the presence of all the celestial love and guidance that always surrounds you, and may your life be filled with magic and miracles.

Part I

Archangels and Angels

Archangels and angels are spiritual beings whose primary function is to act as intermediaries between mortals and God. Angels have fascinated human beings for millennia. They are usually depicted as very graceful and beautiful beings with wings. When someone says, "You're an angel," they usually mean you are a blessing and have probably been very helpful.

Angels are always willing to be of assistance. They love you and want you to be happy. They will never interfere in your life unless you ask for their assistance. Angels can't do anything for you directly, but they can guide you, make suggestions, and help you avoid potential obstacles. In return, they simply ask that you deepen your connection with your spirit and open your heart to the powerful forces of love and gratitude.

Surprisingly, the angelic realms are structured and have hierarchies. Depending on the tradition, there are many levels and numerous categories. The term *archangel* comes from the Greek word *archangelos*, which means chief or eminent messenger. They are also known as the "Holy Ones."

When you are working with the angels, take some time to get to know them. Each one has a unique personality, and each one has an area they excel in. Once you get to know them, you will instinctively know whom to call on. Allow them to become your friends, and become familiar with all of them. Once you develop the habit of calling on them, you will find it becomes almost second nature to acknowledge their presence and welcome their assistance. They are more than willing to help you, so why not let them?

Archangel Michael

Associated Faiths

Judaism / Christianity / Islam

Michael will help you

- Love yourself
- Have the courage of your convictions
- Find your life's purpose

- Improve all of your relationships
- Find a career that makes your heart sing
- Live your life fully and passionately

Invocation

The colors usually associated with Archangel Michael are green and red. He is very easygoing, so you don't really have to do anything special to call upon him other than to ask for his help. Michael usually has a sword that he uses to cut through any resistance, so you can write your request on a piece of paper. Then imagine his sword and tear the letter into small pieces, knowing he has heard your prayer. You can burn the pieces or throw them away.

Archangel Michael is referred to as the greatest of all angels. His name signifies "He who is like God." He is a perfect manifestation of God's mercy and was put in charge of nature, including the rain, snow, wind, thunder, lightning, and clouds. Michael is the archangel of protection and the patron saint of policemen. He facilitates patience, lends courage, helps with career ambitions, and provides motivation to help you accomplish all of life's tasks.

As soon as you invite Michael into your life, you will feel his love and protection. Michael is often pictured holding a sword, which represents courage and his ability to conquer or overcome any obstacle. With his sword he will gladly remove any problem in your path, so call upon him when you feel challenged or stymied. He is enthusiastic and full of energy and will readily take up any task set before him.

It is said that the Archangel Michael appeared to Moses as the fire in the burning bush, rescued Daniel from the lions' den, and informed Mary of her approaching death. Both Gabriel and Michael visited the Prophet Muhammad to teach him of peace. Michael is God's messenger of love, hope, peace, joy, wisdom, and grace. He loves to help anyone who reaches out to him. He helps people to overcome their hopelessness and to easily manifest their deepest dreams.

Archangel Azrael

Associated Faiths

Judaism / Islam

Azrael will help you

- Move smoothly through the process of death and dying
- Ease your grief
- Remove blocks from your spiritual path
- Hear the guidance of your spirit

Invocation

Azrael is often associated with the color purple. You can use a small piece of amethyst when you want to work with him. You can hold it in your hand as you call upon him, carry it with you, or place it somewhere you will see it throughout the day. In times of grief, allow him to enfold you with his wings and comfort you. Ask for his assistance when you feel blocked in your personal life. An effective way to call upon him is to light a small white candle, call out his name, and ask for his assistance.

Azrael's name means "he who helps God" or "messenger." His duty is to help the God (or gods) of various religions. Azrael will help you release anything blocking your spiritual growth.

He is also the angel of death. His main job is to guide people through the death process. Azrael helps them feel safe and secure as they leave this life behind, taking care they don't suffer as they are dying. He helps their spirits adjust to life on the other side. Azrael keeps track of every person who is born and then erases his or her name when that person dies. It is said that a leaf falls from the throne of God when it is time for a person to die. Azrael has forty days to collect the person's soul. He also comforts the grieving family, enfolding them with his huge wings and filling them with his love and healing energy. If you call upon him in a time of grief, he will actually absorb the emotional pain of loss so you can be happy again.

Azrael also teaches mankind the difference between truth and illusion. He brings insights and wisdom to all who ask. In the Muslim tradition, he was one of four angels Allah sent to the Earth to collect soil so he could create Adam. Though the others failed, he brought back enough soil for Allah to bring Adam to life.

Archangel Jehudiel

Associated Faith

Judaism

Jehudiel will help you

- Overcome jealousy and self-doubt
- Find direction in life
- Create harmony
- Have confidence

- Attract a new love
- Get a great job
- Improve your singing ability

Invocation

Ask Jehudiel to help you spring into action. Take a deep breath and call his name. Hold your hands over your heart and imagine a large indigo ball. Fill it with your requests and then throw it up into the air, knowing he will catch it. When you ask him to help you, he will be there for you, now and always.

Jehudiel is the archangel of divine direction. He has a golden crown in his right hand, and in his left he holds three branches representing spring and new life. His name refers to the glory of God. He leads angels in uplifting songs and chants, which help maintain order in the universe and spread harmonic resonance through the celestial spheres.

Jehudiel is a powerful leader who can heal envy and help people develop self-esteem. His lilting voice will remind you of how wonderful you truly are. He sees only God's perfection in each person and in every situation and will help you to do the same.

As the caretaker of spring, he is excellent with new beginnings. So if you are thinking about starting a project, call upon him. He will guide you to success, making the process easy and enjoyable. He can also be called upon for a safe and smooth childbirth.

Jehudiel can also enhance your musical skills. He can bring harmony and balance into any area of your life, including a cluttered home or a messy desk. Is your car a mess? Call on Jehudiel and he will help you make it shine like new. Deep purple is his color and lilacs are his flower. When he is around, you are apt to see flashes of deep indigo or smell the luscious scent of freshly picked lilacs.

Archangel Raguel

Associated Faiths

Judaism / Islam

Raguel will help you

- Create balance
- Smooth out disagreements
- Expose and correct corruption
- Resolve deep-seated issues
- Discover your life's work

Invocation

Raguel loves the flowers of spring because they represent the infinite possibilities of each moment. When you want Raguel's loving guidance and support, put a few of your favorite flowers in a beautiful vase next to a white candle. Light the candle and ask for his assistance. Then allow yourself to become quiet and to listen for his gentle guidance.

Archangel Raguel is the angel of justice, balance, fairness, and harmony. His name means "friend of God." He has the task of making sure angels are doing their jobs properly and are taking loving care of mortals. Raguel is described in the Book of Enoch as the angel in charge of luminaries. Since he brings other angels to task for unangelic behavior, in some texts he is referred to as a demon. In fact, his concern for justice, balance, and harmony precludes him being a force of evil.

As a member of the Order of Principalities, Raguel is responsible for helping nations work together harmoniously. If you suspect corruption in your local government, call upon Raguel and he will help restore balance, making sure fairness and harmony prevail. Raguel also has dominion over ice and snow, so it is useful to call upon him if you are having problems with a winter storm.

Raguel is a loving angel dedicated to manifesting the divine, so he works closely with the beloved deities who are in charge of this magnificent universe. He will gladly help you get in touch with your highest purpose and align yourself with the expansive vista of your possible futures. If you ask for his assistance, he will guide you toward the path that will bring you the greatest happiness and joy.

Archangel Chamuel

Associated Faith

Judaism

Chamuel will help you

- Overcome depression
- Create inner peace
- Improve relationships
- Forgive others and yourself

- Find true love
- Love and accept yourself
- Establish a career

Invocation

Call upon Chamuel for all matters of the heart, both big and small. Imagine yourself bathed in a bright pink light. Open your heart and allow him to guide your thoughts and feelings. Write your hopes, dreams, and desires on pieces of paper, light a pink candle, and burn them. Watch the smoke rise, knowing your requests will be willingly granted by Chamuel.

Chamuel's name means "He who seeks God." He is often described as "pure love in a winged form." He encourages open-mindedness and reminds us that we must love ourselves first if we have any hope of being able to love others. Chamuel will help you release judgmental attitudes, even if you are unaware of them. He will help you use your shortcomings as an opportunity to connect with your spirit, rather than carry them as a burden. He is one of two angels who comforted Jesus in the Garden of Gethsemane.

When you call upon him, you may see a ray of pink light. Chamuel will help you develop compassion, improve your ability to communicate, balance your life, and understand the value of helping others. When you feel lost or overwhelmed, call upon him. Chamuel will help you heal family dysfunctions and overcome grief. He assists with love, relationships, creativity, and spirituality. He helps to improve existing relationships and will help you find your soul mate. He will also assist you in building a strong, long-lasting foundation for your relationships and your career.

When Chamuel is around, you will feel a warm, tingling sensation in your body. He will help you open your heart and forgive after a bitter divorce or the tragic death of a loved one.

Archangel Zaphiel

Associated Faith

Judaism

Zaphiel will help you

- Regulate the weather
- Find inner peace
- Heal an injured animal
- Sleep better
- Protect your children
- Fill your heart with forgiveness

Invocation

Light a pale blue candle before you call upon him. First, ask for the ability to forgive yourself and all those involved with the issue, even if you do not see the need for forgiveness. Then, with great humility, ask for his help. The moment you open your heart and your mind to him, he will do everything in his power to help you resolve the problem.

Zaphiel is the leader of the choir of cherubim. His voice possesses the power and strength to soften even the angriest of hearts. His robes are made of the finest pale blue silk. Although humble, he carries himself with dignity. His smile is magnificent. As Noah's personal guide, he saved Noah's family, instructing them as they built the ark and teaching them how to withstand the great flood. He is tender and cares for all beings, even the smallest of animals. Zaphiel values forgiveness and humility and will show you how to see the love and perfection in any situation.

When you call upon him, he will joyously embrace you and remove any doubt or fear you may have about the future. Once you put your life in divine hands and are willing to follow the insights you receive, magic and miracles will become part of your everyday life.

Zaphiel is especially fond of children and will gladly help them. If your child is struggling in any way, teach her or him to ask for Zaphiel's help. Perhaps before you tuck your children into bed, you can sit together and ask for Zaphiel's assistance. He will enfold them in his wings and smooth out some of life's speed bumps. If the weather has been too wet or too dry, call upon him to create balance and harmony. He is known for his miracles, and he is a good friend to have.

Archangel Gabriel

Associated Faiths

Judaism / Islam / Christianity

Gabriel will help you

- Connect with your feminine side
- Receive a message from your spirit
- Celebrate your life
- Manifest your deepest desire
- Cleanse your body, mind, home, and spirit
- Be protected in violent weather or in travel
- Communicate with your unborn child

Invocation

Gabriel's voice will fill you with peace and joy. When you see moonlight streaming into your home, know Gabriel is there, willing to bless you with his presence.

A simple request is all Gabriel requires: "Gabriel, I ask for your guidance and assistance. Please help me [explain your needs]. I give thanks for your love and for being in my life."

Gabriel stands in the presence of God and is one of the two highest-ranking angels. He is a messenger whose symbol is the trumpet. Gabriel buried Moses and dictated the Koran to the prophet Mohammed. He announced the birth of John the Baptist to the world and told Mary she would give birth to Jesus. Gabriel brings a message of hope to mankind. He reminds everyone of the importance of loving one another. He encourages unity and oneness. He brings mercy, forgiveness, change, and transformation.

Gabriel is associated with the moon. He often makes his presence known with a flash of silver light. He also rules the element of water and is associated with the direction of the west. He helps with intuitive insights, herbal medicine, and women's menstrual cycles. Gabriel also chooses which souls will be born. He spends nine months with the baby's spirit, helping the spirit adjust to the exciting journey of life on earth. When the child is born, he causes the child to forget the secrets of heaven by pressing his finger below the baby's nose. This creates the cleft in a human's upper lip.

Gabriel has the ability to grant wishes, bring joy, unveil divine mysteries, reveal truth, and grant justice. Gabriel can protect you from violent weather and make your travel easy and effortless.

Archangel Sariel

Associated Faiths

Judaism / Islam / Christianity

Sariel will help you

- Understand symbolism
- See the magic in all of life
- Expand your ability to love
- Create loving relationships
- Use your dreams for guidance

Invocation

Sariel loves the flute, so put on some flute music and then sit back and listen until you feel relaxed and open. You might say, "Sariel, fill me with your magic. Help me connect with my inner wisdom and be in alignment with my spirit. Show me the way. Please help me, and I give thanks."

Sariel is an archangel who taught men about women's cycles and the power of the phases of the moon. In the Book of Enoch, he is called the "light of God" or, alternately, "the light of the moon." Sariel stands at the gateway between waking and sleeping consciousness. He is in charge of our dreams and will help you interpret your dreams. He will remind you of your inherent wisdom and teach you about accessing and embracing your own symbolism. Sariel has an immense knowledge of magic. As a magical angel of the night, he assists humans in connecting with their sexuality.

In Hebrew and Christian traditions, he was a warrior, and his name was often inscribed on soldiers' shields. Yet

Sariel values peace most highly, and when you call upon him, you will immediately feel safe and peaceful. He will encourage self-control, courage, and tolerance within you. He will plant the seeds of forgiveness and acceptance in your heart and encourage them to blossom and grow.

Whenever you are in transition, call upon Sariel and he will guide your thoughts and actions. After you ask for his guidance, be sure to pay attention to your dreams and the subtle messages in your days. Go outside into the night and allow the light of the moon to fill your heart and your mind. Allow yourself to feel his presence. He will be there for you now and always.

Archangel Remiel

Associated Faith

Judaism

Remiel will help you

- Connect with your inner guidance
- Find love
- Work with your dreams

- Relieve depression
- Let go of anything that no longer serves you

Invocation

To invite the power of Remiel, just call his name. The color associated with him is silvery white and his favorite flower is the gardenia. If you want to work closely with him, get a gardenia-scented white candle and light it before you invoke him.

Remiel is the "Angel of Hope," responsible for divine visions. In the Book of Enoch, he is identified as one of the seven archangels who stand closest to God. He also guides souls into heaven and is one of the angels God is most likely to send to beings in distress. His name roughly translates as "God's mercy." He will bring harmony into your life.

When Remiel is near, you are likely to hear the rumble of distant thunder. He is a very powerful angel, so call upon him only if you are serious about making changes. Before you go to sleep at night, set your intention to remember your dreams, and then call on Remiel. Pay attention to your dreams and notice what kind of mes-

sages Remiel has sent to you. If you don't understand the symbolism in the dream, ask him for clarification before you go to sleep the next night.

If you are having doubts about your spirituality or are struggling to deepen your spiritual connection, ask Remiel for help. He will enfold you with his golden wings and surround you with an intense feeling of love and connection. Surrender to his presence and see what kind of magic and miracles happen in your life.

Remiel is a magnificent angel surrounded with a brilliant white light. He has deep brown eyes and golden hair. He will move gracefully through your life, bringing balance, wisdom, and joy.

Archangel Ariel

Associated Faith

Judaism

Ariel will help you

- Heal an injured animal
- Bring greater harmony into all of your relationships
- Bless your home
- Overcome environmental concerns
- Cleanse and purify your home and body

Invocation

When you want Ariel's assistance, whisper his name into the wind or when standing near running water. If you are dealing with an injured animal, invoke the healing powers of both Ariel and Raphael. Since Ariel is a master of manifestation, ask him to help you bring forth your deepest dreams.

Archangel Ariel is deeply connected to Mother Earth. He is a master at creating balance and harmony in even the most chaotic situations. In the Kabbalah, Ariel is closely associated with releasing trapped spirits, manifestation, and divine magic.

His name means "lion of God." When he is near, you will often see a bright, golden light or feel the presence of a lion. He is deeply committed to healing and protecting nature, especially wild animals, birds, and fish. If you find an injured animal, call upon Ariel. He will work together with Raphael to heal the animal. Ariel can be invoked to heal disease in people as well.

Ariel is also a water spirit and is in charge of "sprites," those angels associated with water. He has a deep connection to the whales, dolphins, and sea turtles. His presence is especially strong when you are near running water or the ocean. He is also associated with the wind.

Ariel is an expert at cleansing and purifying. Call upon him if you want to bless your house or make your garden flourish. Whenever you want to spruce up a room or do spring cleaning, ask Ariel for his assistance. To be assured of his presence in your home, set up a small fountain and place a few plants around it.

Archangel Jophiel

Associated Faiths

Judaism / Christianity

Jophiel will help you

- Do well on exams
- Clean the house
- Overcome ignorance
- Banish prejudice
- Protect the environment
- Jazz up your spiritual practices
- Enhance your creativity

Invocation

Ask archangel Jophiel to inspire you. He often works in subtle ways, so don't be discouraged if you don't see instantaneous results. He is there, bringing his wisdom and insight into your life. Although his help may seem slow in manifesting, he works at a profound level to bring about permanent change and lasting solutions.

Light a yellow or gold candle when you ask for Jophiel's assistance.
Take a few minutes to gather your thoughts, then talk to him about your life.
Allow his gentleness and joy to illuminate all of your choices.

Jophiel is believed to be the first angel mentioned in the Bible. His name means "Beauty of God." He guards the Tree of Life with a flaming sword and drove Adam and Eve from the Garden of Eden, freeing them so they could experience life more fully. His fiery sword cuts through illusion.

He is often associated with the color yellow. Jophiel wears a silver tunic and has warm, penetrating blue eyes. His large, shimmering wings cast a soft golden light over everything near them. Jophiel will help you manifest joy and happiness, illuminate your life, and see the beauty around you. Jophiel blesses all creative endeavors and extends possibilities to those who call on him.

Jophiel teaches about love and the power of light within creation. He is in the choir of cherubim, where his sweet voice reminds you of the magnificence of spiritual pursuits. He brings inner wisdom, illumination, and consistency.

Archangel Haniel

Associated Faith

Judaism

Haniel will help you

- Make new friends
- Create an outrageous love life
- Enhance any artistic endeavors

- Heighten your intuition
- Enliven your healing rituals
- Bring balance into all areas of your life

Invocation

If you want Haniel to help you develop your spiritual gifts, light a silver candle. To facilitate physical healing, burn a green candle. A deep magenta candle will help evoke divine grace. Then stand in the light of the moon and call her name. She will be there in an instant to fill you with the wisdom, strength, and abundance of divine grace.

Archangel Haniel is also called the "glory of the grace of God." She is an angel of principalities, and in that role she is the caregiver of all nations on Earth. She is empowered with a great deal of wisdom and strength and can directly impact human affairs. When called upon, Haniel can change the hearts and minds of world leaders to bring about significant changes for the benefit of humanity. She is able to turn barren ground into fertile and productive land. In an instant, Haniel can change your mood from one of great hopelessness to one of great joy.

Haniel wears an emerald green robe and has large silver-gray wings. She is often seen carrying a luminescent brown lantern. She brings harmony and balance wherever she goes. Her symbol, the rose, represents the beauty of spiritual growth. She will help you embrace your spiritual gifts by drawing upon the energy of the moon. She will also facilitate physical, emotional, and spiritual healing.

Haniel radiates inner wisdom and strength, which she willingly imparts to anyone who calls upon her. She also imbues people with common sense and is wonderful to invite in times of discord. Haniel reminds you to find fulfillment from within rather than trying to find happiness from outside yourself. She reminds humans that external joy is fleeting, while the happiness that comes from within is never lost.

Archangel Zadkiel

Associated Faith

Judaism

Zadkiel will help you

- Fill your life with freedom and grace
- Feel comfort in your darkest hours
- Move from one perfect moment to the next
- Be of service to yourself and the world
- Improve your memory

Invocation

Zadkiel is very easy to work with. You can simply call his name and light your favorite candle, or you could say: "Zadkiel, most sacred of all angels, please guide me and direct me with your wisdom. Show me how to love all of life and release any judgments I have about myself or others. Help me experience the perfection and divine nature of each moment of life. I give thanks for all of your assistance."

Zadkiel is an angel of mercy whose name means "righteousness of God." He is one of the nine rulers of heaven and one of the seven archangels who stand next to God.

He reminds people that God is benevolent, infusing the world with a deep sense of divine perfection. If you want to drastically change your experience of life, Zadkiel will assist you in becoming aligned with this perfection. He brings comfort, gentleness, freedom, and grace into the lives of anyone who asks for his help.

Zadkiel works with cellular memory to deepen your connection with your divine nature. He reminds all mortals of their immortality. Once you remember you are an eternal and infinite being, you can make all of your choices based on love instead of fear.

You can pray to Zadkiel when in need of guidance, comfort, or encouragement. He guards the most powerful form of invocation—he protects prayer from misuse. He reminds us that prayer is the most powerful means of opening to our true nature and connecting with the sacred beings we are.

Archangel Jeremiel

Associated Faith

Judaism

Jeremiel will help you

- Engage your innate wisdom
- Find easy solutions for even the most difficult problems
- Manifest your dreams

- Deepen your ability to experience compassion
- Create an incredible future

Invocation

Ask Jeremiel for his assistance and he will be there for you. He has such a big heart and a deep desire to help that you really don't have to do anything special. But if you wish, you can light a purple candle and say a simple prayer.

Jeremiel's name means "Mercy of God." He guides anyone who calls upon him with his gentle, powerful, and profound sense of tenderness and lovingkindness. Archangel Jeremiel allows positive adjustments in thoughts and behaviors to become a natural part of everyday life. He is the angel of insights and visions. He helps people who have just died to review their lives. Jeremiel will also help you to take an inventory of your life and amplify what works while releasing anything that no longer serves you.

Jeremiel is a visionary. He will help you manifest your dreams and enhance your dream life. When he is around, you will see flashes of a deep purple that is almost black, like the skin of an eggplant. If you have any concerns about the future, call upon him. He will guide you with love and make sure that life's lessons are presented in a most gentle manner.

Since Jeremiel inspires mercy, he will help you create harmony in all aspects of your life. He will inspire you to attain your highest goals, find your inner wisdom, and preserve knowledge that will be of service to you and to all of mankind. He motivates people to be of service because he knows that in doing so we find our greatest happiness.

Once you invite Jeremiel into your life, your perspective will never be the same. Your thoughts will become clearer and your discernment impeccable. You will see life from a loving and compassionate perspective rather than from a fear-based, judgmental one.

Archangel Raphael

Associated Faiths

Judaism / Christianity

Raphael will help you

- Travel with ease and safety
- Heal your mind, body, or spirit
- Clarify your thinking
- Make decisions
- See life's endless possibilities
- Do well on your exams

Invocation

Simply ask for Raphael's help, and he will be there for you.
You could say something like, "Raphael, angel of healing, shine brightly in my life.
I thank you in advance for your guidance, love, and protection."

Raphael's name means "God heals." He is one of the seven angels who have dominion over the Earth. Above all, Archangel Raphael is dedicated to healing. Raphael will supply the energy needed to overcome any challenges in your life. He can heal relationships and bring you profound insights. He carries a huge sword, which will enable you to cut through illusion. Raphael responds to prayer, bringing joy, love, peace, and miracles to anyone who calls upon him. If you have a sudden impulse to pray, you can be sure Raphael is inviting you to speak with him.

Raphael is associated with spring and the evening wind. He can be called upon to assist in healing the Earth.

He also protects children and travelers, guiding those who take both outward and inward journeys. He is charged with guiding the sun as it travels on its heavenly journey. He will guide you as well. Ask Raphael to help you alleviate physical or emotional pain and he will.

Raphael's robes are made of the softest golden silk. When he enters your life, you may feel a gentle breeze or see his robe blowing in the wind. Raphael will give you the courage to explore the unknown within yourself and in the world around you. He facilitates breakthroughs in the academic world. He will help you see your limiting beliefs, agreements, and assumptions with clarity so that you can let go of them.

Archangel Zerachiel

Associated Faith

Judaism

Zerachiel will help you

- Release addictions
- Find lost objects and pets
- Heal
- Succeed at gardening projects

- Work with your dreams
- Overcome insomnia
- Come to terms with childhood traumas

Invocation

A simple request will immediately bring Zerachiel to your aid.
He is a great listener, so pour out your heart to him. His loving
presence will guide you to the better times right around the corner.

Zerachiel is one of the seven archangels named in the Book of Enoch. He is an angel of healing who watches over human beings, especially those children whose parents have problems with addictions. Zerachiel understands that children raised in such homes need extra love and support. He embraces them with his wings and whispers words of encouragement to them while they sleep. If you have problems with night terrors or falling asleep, Zerachiel will help you. He will also help you work with your dreams.

He has dominion over the Earth and tenderly takes care of the environment and animals of all kinds. Call upon his healing power immediately if one of your pets falls ill. If your beloved pet gets lost, Zerachiel will help you find him.

Zerachiel helps with memory. He is a great angel to call on before you take an exam, when you need to remember a person's name, or when you're trying to find an object, such as your keys.

When he is around, you will probably see flashes of burgundy or deep purple. His robes are bordered in gold, and he wears a golden belt. He is regal in bearing and has a soft, loving, and kind face. When you call on him, you will feel a gentle warmth spreading across your chest. Your hands and feet might tingle. Zerachiel may whisper to you in your dreams. You may even find yourself turning left when you meant to go right. Trust the process, and know he is guiding you. If, for example, you get an urge for a cup of exotic coffee, go to your favorite coffeehouse, and expect to find the answer to your problems there.

Archangel Uriel

Associated Faiths

Uriel will help you

- Tap into your creativity
- Deepen your insights into life
- See the variety of futures your choices create
- Make your choices based on love
- Transform even your worse nightmare into a gift

Invocation

Since Uriel is the angel of creativity, one way to ask for his help is to write him a letter. You can address it to Uriel and mail it, burn it, or simply throw it away. Writing is a wonderful way to focus your thoughts and release your prayers. You can also make a storyboard. Cut out pictures that represent what you want to create, write Uriel's name on the top, and at the bottom write, "Help me create this or something better." Then hang the storyboard someplace you'll see it. Spend a few minutes looking at it each day, knowing that Uriel is working his magic.

Uriel is the angel of creativity and prophecy. He is a magnificent angel with glistening silver wings. Uriel is listed as both a cherub and seraph and has a long list of titles, including "regent of the sun" and "angel of presence." He has a passion for music, prophecy, and the salvation of all human beings. He is known for his deep commitment to fulfilling divine will and for his ability to find unusual creative solutions to any problem.

Uriel's name means "fire of God." According to the Book of Enoch, he is the angel with dominion over thunder and terror. Angelic lore is rich in stories about Uriel. In one myth, Uriel showed how the capacity for discernment, of seeing through an open heart, invited divine grace. Through teaching people how to see life through the eyes of love, he is able to impart profound insights about life's journey. As an angel of salvation and transformation, Uriel brings peace and can turn your most challenging and painful experiences into your greatest blessings.

Uriel is very gracious and willing to help mortals in any way possible. When he is around, you might see images of midnight blue. With his love he teaches people the difference between listening to the limiting beliefs of the mind and living the expansive perspective of the spirit.

Suriel

Associated Faith

Judaism

Suriel will help you

- Connect with your inner wisdom
- Protect your home and your possessions
- Develop a green thumb and have a gorgeous garden
- Stay on your spiritual path
- Manifest your deepest desires

Invocation

Since Suriel is an angel of healing, he has the ability to help you let go of limiting beliefs that no longer serve you. He can help you change old constricting behaviors into new expansive experiences.

Suriel will often announce his presence with a flash of purple light. He is a benevolent and loving angel, so simply open your heart to his power and wisdom and ask for his help.

Suriel is an angel of healing and is also known as a loving and benevolent angel of death. He was the source of Moses's incredible knowledge. In recognition of their bond, God sent Suriel to escort Moses's soul into heaven.

Suriel has power over the primordial elements. He helps to determine and control the position of the fixed stars. When you go out at night, take a moment to look up at the stars. Suriel will help you feel the balance and beauty of the universe and remind you that you are part of that wonderful system of perfection

Sometimes when he is invoked, he appears in the shape of a great white ox. In the Kabbalah, he is named as one of the angels who rules over Earth. Suriel is also considered an angel of protection. He can help protect your home and beautify your garden. He will help you feel the presence of love in your life.

Suriel has the ability to manifest anything from nothing. He will show you how to focus your mind so you can harness your own inner creativity. He will help you express your divinity so you can transform any of your limitations into incredible assets. Call upon him often, and he will show you how to create a life beyond your wildest imaginings.

Miniel

Associated Faith

Mysticism

Miniel will help you

- Deepen your experience of love
- Find a new job
- Care for nature
- Create a new career

Invocation

Face south when you call upon Miniel for love. Be clear about your purpose.
Rather than asking that a specific person love you, it is far better to ask to experience
romance, love, and companionship and then let Miniel work his magic.

Miniel also resonates with the moon. When the moon is new, plant the seeds of what
you would like to create in the coming month. At the full moon, ask Miniel to help you
release any beliefs or behaviors that stop you from experiencing love in your life.

Miniel is the angel of love, well known in magical circles. He can be invoked when you want someone to fall in love with you. Miniel can't make anyone love you, but he can help you radiate the expansive beauty of your spirit, which is pretty irresistible. He will remind you that love is about freely sharing. If you try to control or smother another person, he will quickly show you the price of such fear-based behavior. After all, the best way to experience love in your life is to freely share your love with everyone.

Miniel also helps protect wild animals from becoming extinct. When you are walking in a wild preserve or see a disturbing segment on TV about wildlife, call upon Miniel. As more people ask Miniel to protect endangered animals, his blessings will help these animals to flourish again. So call upon Miniel often, to protect this beautiful planet we call home and to bring more love to our lives.

Gadiel

Associated Faith

Judaism

Gadiel will help you

- Maintain a positive outlook
- Repair a damaged relationship
- Improve your job performance
- Transform your life
- Release limiting beliefs
- Create abundance

Invocation

One way to call upon Gadiel is to go outside when the wind is blowing. Invite the wind to carry your prayers to him. His name has great power, so saying "Gadiel" repeatedly while you ask for his assistance is also a wonderful way to invite him closer.

You can also close your eyes and imagine that your request is tied to a beautiful balloon. Take a few deep breaths, and when the time feels right, imagine letting go of the balloon. Know that Gadiel will always answer your prayers.

Gadiel is called the most holy of angels. His name means "God is my wealth." He is one of several guards of the gate of the south wind. His name has been found inscribed on amulets used to ward off evil. Sorcerers often invoke Gadiel to conjure up great power.

When you call upon Gadiel, you may see flashes of yellow or green. You may also see your curtains stirring even though the windows are closed. Trust his love to point you toward the truth and show you the best direction for you to take in your life.

If you are feeling down or victimized by life, Gadiel is the angel to call upon. Before you confront any negative situation, ask for his protection. Gadiel will also help you release any negative feelings you have after a disagreement with a friend, an unfavorable assessment from a boss, or an argument with a lover. He is so full of love that he will help you let go of anything that is less than unconditionally loving.

Elim

Associated Faith

Judaism

Elim will help you

- Ease menstrual pain
- Transition easily through menopause
- Create a loving home
- Call in abundance

Invocation

Imagine you are standing in the high desert under the pristine night sky.
The wind is cool and gritty as it travels over the expanses of sand. The smell of sage lingers
in the air. Take a deep breath and ask for Elim's assistance. The twinkling of the stars will
bring you the confirmation that he is by your side, supporting you and guiding your way.

If you want to call him into your home, burn some sage or light a sand-colored candle. Placing a sage
potpourri in the drawer where you keep your bills will attract the abundance to easily pay them.

Elim belongs to a high order of angels. His name has been translated as "the mighty ones," "gods," "heavenly being," and "holy one." A variation of his name also refers to a sacred place in the high desert as well as to a type of palm tree. Elim is the guardian of the night who maintains the celestial spheres in perfect harmony. He is the angel of the moon, and he will bring the magic and wisdom of moon cycles into your life.

Elim's presence is most acute at the new moon, when the sky is darkest. Elim's lessons unfold with the monthly cycle of the moon. At the full moon, Elim will help to illuminate your shadow self. When the moon is new, he will help you transform your shadow self into the creative source it was always meant to be.

Women can call upon Elim to regulate their monthly cycles and to assist in making menopause a gentle and easy journey.

Ohrmazd

Associated Culture

Persian

Ohrmazd will help you

- Solve any dilemma
- Overcome any legal issues
- Access your inner wisdom
- Release negativity
- Bless a new endeavor
- Bless your home
- Protect your family

Invocation

When you close your eyes and call upon Ohrmazd, you are likely to see a bright explosion of white light. Freely ask his assistance with any area of your life as long as you are being honest, loving, and kind. He is dedicated to love and to divine justice.

You might say, "Ohrmazd, help me let go of any limiting beliefs or behaviors. Shower me with your love so I feel safe enough to be vulnerable, open, and loving with everyone, regardless of how they are behaving. Allow me to be a beacon of love, light, and laughter."

Ohrmazd is a magnificent being of light who is considered to be both an angel and a deity. He shimmers with brilliant lights and flashes of violet, pink, and purple. He is a powerful source of goodness who refuses to allow evil. If you are angry with someone and want to get even, he will show you the dire consequences loveless behaviors create. Love is always the answer. Ohrmazd will always apply the healing balm of love to all areas of your life.

Ohrmazd is a symbol of hope and a messenger of wisdom. He can transform even the most dismal situation into one of great healing. Ohrmazd will right any wrongs and find an equitable solution to any problem. He possesses great wisdom and is an incredibly creative being of light. When Ohrmazd appears in your life, the world will seem brighter and miracles will become commonplace.

Ministering Angels

Associated Faith

Judaism

Ministering angels will help you

- Heal physically, emotionally, mentally, or spiritually
- Find guidance and direction

- Give comfort to a loved one
- Overcome hardships during times of disasters or great violence

Invocation

It is wonderful to start your day by calling upon your Ministering angels. Place a beautiful piece of cloth in a place where the morning sun will fall upon it. Find a glass that will sparkle in the sunlight. Each morning fill the glass with water and take a moment or two to ask the Ministering angels to guide and protect you for the day. Before you go to bed, take a moment to give thanks for another wonderful day and empty the glass. As you pour out the water, visualize yourself sleeping soundly and awakening renewed and refreshed. If you are feeling ill, hold a glass of water in your hand and ask for the healing of your Ministering angels. Imagine their love and healing energy pouring into the water and then drink it.

Ministering angels are created each morning to bring gratitude, comfort, and joy into the universe and are reabsorbed into the divine ethers every evening. These angels minister to any being in need of divine assistance. In some traditions they are considered the highest order of angel, while in other systems they are considered to be at the bottom of the angel hierarchy.

It isn't clear how many Ministering angels there are, but when you need the services of one, rest assured there are more than enough of them to go around. Although nameless, they are a very powerful force of healing and come readily when they are invited. When you awaken in the morning, ask for their guidance, love, and direction. If you are feeling ill, ask them to heal your physical body.

Emmanuel

Associated Faiths

Judaism / Christianity

Emmanuel will help you

- Celebrate all of life
- Use gratitude as a gateway to personal freedom
- Transform any situation
- Create healthier relationships

Invocation

Emmanuel is always available to assist you. Once you decide to ask for his assistance, know in your heart of hearts that he has already cleared the way for magic to occur. Focus on being grateful for his loving support.

Then light an orange candle and say, "Emmanuel, help me know what I need to do to experience abundance, happiness, joy, and ease in all areas of my life. Surround me with your love so I can feel your gentle guidance and strength. I give thanks for the miracles that are about to occur in my life."

Emmanuel is loosely translated as "God is with us." He often carries a long sword that opens multidimensional windows through which magic and miracles can travel. He is often mistaken for Metatron, the angel who saved three condemned holy men from a fiery furnace. Emmanuel's name is also sometimes used to identify otherwise nameless angels.

Emmanuel loves the color orange as well as fresh flowers. Butterflies often appear when you call upon him. You will feel the gentle stirring of love, hope, and joy in your heart immediately. Emmanuel reminds us that God is within everyone and everything and that magic and miracles can become part of everyday life if we are willing to allow them.

Emmanuel will remind you to celebrate every moment and to see the sacred in the mundane. Just as a caterpillar becomes a chrysalis and then transforms into a beautiful butterfly, he will help you to revamp your life in miraculous ways. When you call upon Emmanuel, expect to be asked to go within and to deepen your self-understanding.

Jaoel

Associated Faith

Judaism

Jaoel will help you

- Overcome addictions
- Deepen your ability to be compassionate

- See choices and choose among them
- Know the future

Invocation

Jaoel will gladly take you on a journey during your meditations, just as he did for Abraham. Allow yourself to go into a deep meditation and ask Jaoel to guide you. He will show you images of your possible futures so you can decide which course of action would best serve you. Remember, if you see events that frighten or upset you, you can make different choices in the present moment and change your future. If you want Jaoel's assistance and guidance, imagine his wings enfolding you and then just talk to him. He will act like a loving big brother, offering advice and helping to keep you safe.

Jaoel is the keeper of the unspeakable name of God. The images of Jaoel and the cherubim Zarall were said to be carved on the Ark of the Covenant. The shadow of his wings falls over the seat of mercy on the side of the ark. Jaoel guided Abraham on a journey to Paradise where Abraham was shown the course of human history. Jaoel is often associated with Archangel Michael, and their blessings are intertwined. Jaoel is also the singer of eternal praises whose massive wings will protect you.

Jaoel's soft voice will overcome even the strongest resistance. He will encourage you to open yourself to the endless possibilities of life while lovingly pointing out how your thinking stops you from having everything you want. Jaoel understands human beings and feels great compassion for the human condition, while seeing what is truly possible for them.

Barakiel

Associated Faiths

Judaism / Christianity

Barakiel will help you

- Create abundance
- Be protected during a thunderstorm
- Lift your spirits
- Have a positive attitude
- Succeed when it seems like a long shot

Invocation

Barakiel loves the forest, so if you want his aid, light pine, cedar, or sandalwood incense, or place some leaves from your favorite tree around the room. Focus on your request, think clearly about what you want, and then simply ask Barakiel to help you create it. Barakiel loves laughter, so fill your heart with joy and celebration for what is about to come into your life.

Barakiel's name means "God's blessing." He is an ancient angel, more than 130,000 years old, and is considered to be one of God's mightiest angels. According to *The Almadel of Solomon*, a seventeenth-century book purportedly written by King Solomon, Barakiel is in charge of people's attitudes and protects innocents. Barakiel hunts evil, has dominion over lightning, and rules the month of February. He is a ruler of the seraphim, which are divine creatures associated with cherubim. Cherubim are the winged creatures, or guardian spirits, who protected the Garden of Eden.

Barakiel assists people in having a positive outlook and in experiencing good fortune. Gamblers who really want to win would do well to ask Barakiel for his assistance.

Barakiel has a great sense of humor and inspires laughter and joy. It is said that as he walks in his favorite place, the prayers of people appear on the trunks of the trees. He always answers prayers offered with an open heart and a willing spirit.

Camael

Associated Faiths

Judaism / Druid

Camael will help you

- Create balance
- Release stress
- Awaken your innate goodness

- Find justice
- Succeed in any venture
- Improve your relationships

Invocation

Light a green candle, take a few deep breaths, and allow Camael to
surround you with his magnificent wings. Open your heart and ask
for his assistance. Honestly express your wants, needs, and desires.
Allow yourself to feel his love and to be guided by his wisdom.

Camael's name refers to "divine justice." He wrestled with Jacob and appeared to Jesus in the Garden of Gethsemane, filling him with hope at a time of great despair. In Druid mythology, he is the god of war and rules the planet Mars. When invoked, he can appear as a leopard crouching on a rock or as a warrior dressed in a red tunic. He wears a green vest and has huge green wings. When you call upon him, you will often see flashes of green.

Camael is the gatekeeper of heaven. He bestows power and invincibility on anyone who asks and who truly loves God. He awakens the goodness or Holiness that exists within everyone. He deepens interpersonal relationships and assists with self-discipline. As a champion of divine justice, Camael is also an arbitrator of karma. He can show you how to release any lingering karma. He can also make sure justice is served if he feels you are being honest.

The greatest gifts in life come when you find the balanced middle way that lies within. When you want to find that balance, call upon Camael. He will help you connect with your inner wisdom and balance all areas of your life so that stress becomes a thing of the past. He will help you take flight and succeed in any endeavor that supports the greatest good.

Gamaliel

Associated Faith

Judaism

Gamaliel will help you

- Find a parking space
- Have more money
- Buy the perfect gift
- Recover a lost object
- Experience more happiness and joy

Invocation

Imagine yourself surrounded by indigo.
Take a few deep breaths, then say something like this:

"Gamaliel, most gracious of angels, I give thanks for your ongoing presence in my life. I know you are always a thought away. Now I ask for your help with [explain your request]. I give thanks for the miracles you are about to perform."

Gamaliel is known as the "recompense" of God, the gracious gift giver. He is often associated with Gabriel and is one of the most generous angels. You are likely to see a deep purple, blue, or indigo color when he is near. One of Gamaliel's missions is to escort honorable people to heaven.

Graciously protecting those who call upon him is his specialty. If you have always loved purple, chances are he has been hovering around, waiting for you to ask for his assistance. Gamaliel is an ancient angel dating back to the beginning of time. Don't allow his lyrical, soft-spoken voice to fool you; he is extremely powerful and very efficient.

Gamaliel can help you create heaven on Earth. Heaven and hell are only a thought away. When you ask for his assistance, he will show you how to change your thinking so you can experience a heavenly life. Ask him to help you whenever you have a decision to make, and watch your life transform before your eyes.

He also specializes in materializing unexpected presents. Thank him next time you find a parking space in a crowded parking lot or someone anonymously pays your toll or you find money. He is a real miracle worker.

Pesagniyah

Associated Faith

Judaism

Pesagniyah will help you

- Overcome the loss of a loved one
- Lift profound sorrow from your heart
- Release emotions from an abusive past
- Forgive the unforgivable

Invocation

When you want to call upon Pesagniyah, clap three times, call his name, and then speak your request out loud. You can also use the following guided meditation: Imagine yourself walking along the shore of a beautiful lake. The sun has just set and the full moon is slowly rising. You walk to the end of a dock and sit on the edge. The moonlight creates a long ribbon of light that stops at your feet. The sounds of the night fill you with a deep sense of peace. As you look at the moon, you sense a loving presence moving towards you. You realize it is Pesagniyah. He asks you how he can be of service. You pour out your heart to him and he listens intently. He reassures you he will take care of everything. You give thanks and know he will always be there whenever you need him.

Pesagniyah is a supervisory angel who has profound knowledge of the ethereal planes. He has large iridescent wings that glisten and sparkle like moonlight. He can illuminate the keys to attaining personal freedom and help to release limiting beliefs. Pesagniyah lifts sorrow and brings forgiveness.

He is associated with the direction of the south. He takes the prayers that come from deep grief and sorrow, surrounding them with his love before he carries them to heaven. When you ask for his assistance, you are likely to feel a gentle kiss upon your left cheek.

Pesagniyah can help you communicate with a loved one who has died. He will carry your messages to her or him and help you remember that the love never dies.

Muriel

Associated Faith

Christianity

Muriel will help you

- Find peace
- Heal your pet

- Make your garden grow
- Love, really love, with an open heart

Invocation

Holding a bouquet of your favorite flowers, face south and softly call "Muriel." Repeat her name until you feel her loving presence. Then ask her for her guidance, love, and assistance. Don't be surprised if you are asked to help someone else. Committing random acts of kindness and honoring beauty are the perfect ways to change your life in a profound manner.

Muriel's name means "God's perfume." Her angelic responsibility includes tending the animals and the plants of Earth. She is often depicted with a crown of flowers, which she lovingly places in the river of life. When she is around, you may smell the subtle scent of your favorite flower.

Muriel brings messages of peace and harmony, reminding us that every selfless good deed is rewarded exponentially. Muriel's huge heart will teach you how to love unconditionally.

As you invite Muriel into your life, you become aware of your intuition. If you suddenly find yourself thinking about helping the homeless, follow through. Muriel teaches us that helping others is the path to true happiness. If you really want your life to change, volunteer at a homeless shelter, pull a few weeds from a local park, hang a bird feeder, or become a dog walker at an animal shelter. Reach out to someone else and see what happens to your life. You might just meet your future love or find the job of your dreams as a result of your willing service. At the same time, Muriel teaches to act with an open heart, without expectation of personal gain. Then and only then will your blessings come back to you multiplied.

Guardian Angels

Associated Faiths

Almost all religions

Your guardian angel will help you

- Connect with angelic guidance
- Find direction in your life
- Know you are protected
- Become filled with hope and joy

Invocation

Remember to call upon your guardian angel often. By simply expressing your desire to get to know your guardian angel, you will give yourself the opportunity to develop an incredibly loving, lifelong relationship. You can begin by closing your eyes and visualizing your guardian angel. Imagine what it feels like to know you are standing side by side. What does your angel look like?

Ask your angel what its name is. It might take a while until you are able to see and hear your angel, but if you practice on a regular basis, it will be well worth your effort. All you have to do is say, "Guardian angel, I know you have always been with me. I open my mind and my heart to your presence. Please help me feel your wings around me, hear your words, and feel your love."

Guardian angels are spiritual beings created expressly to guide and direct spirits incarnated into the physical realm. They work with people, animals, plants, and all aspects of the Earth and the universe. Guardian angels protect you, and most importantly, they will guide you and bring you messages from Spirit. Scriptures say angels were created by God because their existence brought him joy. Perhaps it pleases God to have heavenly beings assisting all of his creations.

The idea of guardian angels is found in Judaism, Christianity, and Islam. You are born with at least one guardian angel who watches over you your entire life. From time to time, other guardian angels will come to assist you when you have a particular want or need. Your angel will encourage you to make choices that will create joy and deepen your spiritual connection. They can't take actions for you or stop you from hurting yourself, but they can gently remind you of your perfection. Their greatest pleasure comes from seeing you succeed in life.

If you begin intuitively receiving advice about the stock market or other speculative ventures, chances are it is your mind pretending to be an angel! The advice of guardian angels is always grounded, loving, and risk-free.

Laylah

Laylah will help you

- Have a child
- Sleep more soundly

- Stop having nightmares
- Protect a newborn

Invocation

Laylah is very easy to invoke. Before you go to bed at night, simply call his name. Share your cares and concerns with him and ask for his assistance. Then sleep easy, knowing he is taking care of your problems. Pay attention to your dreams as you may receive messages in them about actions to take and behaviors to change. If you want to conceive a child, light a candle before you make love, and ask Laylah for his help. If you have a hard time falling asleep, imagine him cradling you in his wings as he sings you to sleep.

Laylah's name is derived from the Hebrew word meaning night. He is appointed to protect each person at the time of her or his birth. Laylah is seen as a force of both good and evil, but traditionally evil is often confused with darkness. While Laylah is an angel of the night, his open heart, love, and compassion put him firmly in the camp of the good guys.

Laylah can be called upon to bless any woman who is struggling to have a child. If you want to conceive, call upon Laylah, but be open to all the possibilities, which may include adoption, being a Big Brother or Sister, or even becoming a foster parent. Often the soul's desire to become a parent means there is a child out there who needs your love and guidance.

Laylah has a soothing voice and will willingly lull you to sleep. He has a powerful affinity for babies and will help them thrive and grow. Parents with a sickly newborn can ask him for help. He helps infants to successfully adjust to life in a physical body.

Theliel

Associated Faith

Gnosticism

Theliel will help you

- Find the love of your life
- Call for rain
- Cool off in the middle of a heat wave
- Get rid of excess weight
- Stop smoking

Invocation

When you want Theliel's assistance, find a beautiful blue stone; a piece of lapis or turquoise will work very well. Hold the stone in your hand, ask for Theliel's help, and then put the stone in the sun, in a place where it won't be disturbed and will catch the light. Know that his help is on the way.

Theliel is the angelic prince of love who is invoked in ceremonial magic to summon peace, joy, and happiness. He is associated with the element of water and the direction of the north. His wings are a translucent dark purple in the center with light blue around the edges. Although very muscular, he moves with exceptional grace. His voice is lyrical and he is soft-spoken, belying his great power. When he looks at you, his blue eyes seem to go right through you.

When you call upon Theliel, you are apt to see a raven nearby. If you find a black feather, you will know he has been hovering around you. Patience is key when working with Theliel. He may take his time solving your problem, but his solution will be thorough and long-lasting. If you are looking for someone to share your life with, he will find just the right person for you. If you want a romantic fling, he isn't your man.

Theliel teaches people about intimacy and commitment. He will show you how to use relationships to work through your stickiest issues so you can make choices in your life rather than reacting to the events happening around you. As you deepen your intimacy with yourself, you will find it easier to release unwanted habits and behaviors.

Bath Kol

Associated Faith

Judaism

Bath Kol will help you

- Find forgiveness
- Improve your singing
- Speak with greater clarity

- Decide what you want to create
- See the possibilities your future contains
- Deepen your ability to love

Invocation

To call upon Bath Kol, think about what you want to create, then
sing out your request. Ask for her help and she will be there.

You might say: "Bath Kol, divine daughter of voice, I ask for your assistance. Please
guide me as I move forward in my life. Help me to overcome my judgment and to see life
through the eyes of love. Assist me in making choices that will enrich my life and the
lives of those around me. I give thanks for your understanding, love, and support."

Bath Kol (Bat Qol) is known as the "heavenly voice" or the "daughter of voice." In the Old Testament, she is symbolized by a dove. Bath Kol encourages loving, clear communications. She will assist you in connecting with your spirit and deepening your experience of love. Bath Kol is also the angel of prophecy, offering us the gift of profound insights into the future. You can use those insights when making your choices.

Bath Kol will come to you during a crisis and remind you that this is a safe and loving universe. Her loving wings will enfold you the moment you open your heart and mind to her and ask for her assistance.

Bath Kol can be invoked when you are finding it difficult to forgive someone or to release your judgments about yourself or about a situation. She will show you how to live with grace, ease, and an open heart. She has the most beautiful voice. Allow her celestial voice to fill your heart and mind as she guides you.

Gazardiel

Associated Faith

Judaism

Gazardiel will help you

- Find new beginnings
- Deepen your understanding of an issue
- Release an addiction

- Find a new love
- Create the perfect home
- Get that well-deserved pay raise
- Launch a new career

Invocation

The ideal place to invoke Gazardiel is where you can clearly see the sunrise. Face the sun, and as the first rays of light strike your face, ask for his assistance. If you can't see the sun, then just face toward the east. Then clearly state your problem and ask for Gazardiel to illuminate your way. His support is always gentle and loving yet very powerful. The clarity he imparts is amazing.

Gazardiel is the angel of the east and is often called "the illuminated one." In some Jewish legends, he is responsible for the rising and setting of the sun. He embodies innocence, renewal, and enlightenment. Gazardiel brings illumination and new beginnings to anyone who asks. He often announces his presence with a shaft of beautiful light. The colors most often associated with Gazardiel are those of a fabulous sunrise: buttery yellow, orange, various hues of pink, and purple. When you call upon Gazardiel, your prayers will be carried directly to God.

I am sure you don't doubt that the sun will rise tomorrow. You can be equally sure of Gazardiel's help.

Kabshiel

Associated Faith

Judaism

Kabshiel will help you

- Communicate and live with ease and laughter
- Let go of an abusive relationship
- Learn how to love yourself
- Release addictions
- Ease the pain of grief

Invocation

Before you ask for Kabshiel's guidance, light a yellow candle. On a nice piece of paper write, "Kabshiel, fill me with your divine grace. Answer my prayers, and help me create a life filled with happiness and joy. Help me resolve [explain your problem]. Your compassion can show me solutions beyond my wildest dreams. Please assist me in manifesting them easily and effortlessly." Write this three times and then burn the paper.

Kabshiel is an angel of divine grace. Divine grace is an opportunity to experience the magical and often instantaneous resolution of an issue or a problem. It doesn't require any effort on the recipient's part; grace just happens. Kabshiel confers divine grace upon anyone who calls on him with an open heart and willing mind. He will instantly lift the burden of an addiction, help release an abusive relationship, or mend a broken heart.

Life's journey can be filled with anguish or with joy. The choices we make in the moment dictate what we will experience. Kabshiel is a master at creating laughter and ease, so call upon him frequently as you move through your day. Before a difficult conversation, ask Kabshiel for his assistance. He can show you how to communicate even the most challenging information with ease and good humor, in a way that it will be readily accepted and often even appreciated.

Kabshiel is often associated with manifesting magical outcomes. When you have a particularly difficult situation, connect with him. Let go of your fears and allow him to direct your thoughts and actions.

Zachriel

Associated Faith

Judaism

Zachriel will help you

- Strengthen your memory
- Find lost objects
- Remember names

- Make balancing your checkbook easy
- Do well on exams
- Improve relationships with your family

Invocation

To invite Zachriel into your life, light a purple candle and call his name. Then say, "Zachriel, help me to remember all the blessings and gifts in my life. Please help me remember to speak in a loving and gentle manner. Assist me in bringing your dignity and grace into all areas of my life. Please help me to [explain your desires]. Thank you for listening to my request and for the magic and miracles you are about to unleash in my life." Asking Zachriel to help you see the issues in your life from a more expansive perspective can bring great insight and peace.

Zachriel is the angel who has dominion over memory. His gilded sword cuts through illusion. He is very tall and lanky with long, snow-white hair. He wears a deep purple gown cinched with a broad silver belt and a large silver ring with a beautiful dragon carved into it. When he is thinking, he often strokes his beard.

Zachriel is a record keeper who helps you maintain all of the memories of your life. He will come silently into your life, reminding you of your perfection. He will touch your heart, filling you with contentment, ease, joy, and acceptance. If you can't remember a name or have lost your keys, call on Zachriel. His presence in your life will definitely make everything flow much more smoothly. When you die, he will help you review your life so you can see your strengths and weaknesses.

Take some time getting to know Zachriel. He will enrich your life and help you enjoy the breadth and depth of your experiences. Zachriel will definitely help you remember the good times and understand what choices you can make to improve the difficult ones. He will help smooth out family relationships and unsnarl parent-child issues.

Metatron

Associated Faiths

Judaism / Christianity

Metatron will help you

- Ease your grief
- Deepen your connection to your spirit
- Find peace during times of crisis
- Transform a painful death to a peaceful one
- Send your prayers to heaven

Invocation

When you invoke Metatron, you will see a towering column of fiery red light. As soon as you ask for his help, you feel your connection to your divinity deepen. You may feel a tingling in your hands and feet or a slight tickling sensation on the top of your head. A simple statement like "Metatron, please help me," is all that is needed.

Metatron is the tallest angel in heaven and is considered to be among the most powerful of angels. One of the more dramatic stories about Metatron concerns two evil Egyptian sorcerers who had managed to trick their way into heaven. Michael and Gabriel tried with all their might to expel them, but they were unable to block the sorcerer's magic. Metatron was able to command the sorcerers to leave.

He has been called the chancellor of heaven and the prince of the ministering angels. The meaning of Metatron's name is often debated by biblical scholars. One interpretation is "the one who sits next to God," while another is "guide or messenger." Metatron is mentioned many times in the Bible. He led the children of Israel out of the wilderness. He wrestled with Job, and he stopped Abraham from killing Isaac. He preserves and enhances the link between human beings and the divine.

One of his duties is to sustain human beings, yet in some legends he is considered the angel of death. He lovingly guides children who die prematurely into Paradise and helps them adjust to life there. He relieves the grief of parents who lose children.

Rachmiel

Associated Faith

Judaism

Rachmiel will help you

- Have a safe and painless childbirth
- Create beautiful and powerful ceremonies
- Deepen your ability to be compassionate
- Move easily through rites of passage like menopause and adolescence

Invocation

Rachmiel's favorite color is red. Writing your request on a piece of red paper will assure you of his help. If you are pregnant, wear red clothing as often as possible or buy a bright red bra. To assure an easy birth and a happy life for your baby, put the child's name in a red frame, write "Rachmiel" on the back, and hang it in the nursery. You can surround the name with images that fill you with joy and give you feelings of hope and abundance. You can also write your prayers on small pieces of paper and hang them on a wind chime in the east. Each time the wind rings the chimes, your prayers will be set free.

Rachmiel is an ancient angel of compassion whose name means mercy and who is known for his very loving heart. He is one of the best angels to call upon during childbirth. He is invoked in ceremonies that honor rites of passage and is one of the angelic guards of the gate of the east wind.

Rachmiel is also often thought of as a savior for lost causes. When all else has failed, call upon him. He will surprise you with his creative solutions. Spend time outside and listen to the wind. Don't be surprised if the answer to your problem blows by on a scrap of paper or if the book you are reading suddenly opens to a page where you experience an ah-ha moment.

Domiel

Associated Faith

Judaism

Domiel will help you

- Find a new home
- Heal a broken bone or mend a broken heart
- Find concrete solutions
- Love yourself and accept your body
- See the magic in the mundane
- Laugh and have fun in the face of adversity

Invocation

Take a few moments and think about the situation you want Domiel's help with. Face north and state the problem. Next turn toward the east and ask him to help you release any attachment to the situation. Then face south and affirm what you want to experience instead. Make sure your statements are positive and an affirmation about what you do want rather than saying what you no longer want. When you finish expressing what you want, say, "I would like this or something better that would benefit myself and all others involved." Then face west and give thanks for the successful resolution of the issue.

Domiel rules the four elements and is often called the "Prince of Majesty." Domiel is magnificent, graceful, and joyous. He sees the goodness and glory in everything. Having dominion over the four directions allows him to fully connect with the Earth and enhances his understanding of the human condition. Domiel will assist you in being grounded and feeling centered. He facilitates the right use of will and will assist in empowering you to deepen your heavenly connection.

Sometimes he's confused with Duma, the interrupter of dreams.

Domiel is very easy to talk to, and his solutions are always very practical and fun. He is a delightful angel to get to know. Even though he is very well grounded, he will show you how to laugh and to have a great time while you move through life. He can help you to enjoy even the most boring tasks, so call on him frequently.

Israfil

Israfil will help you

- Write music
- Increase your musical abilities
- Experience the power of gratitude

- Heal an old wound or injury
- Alleviate depression

Invocation

To evoke Israfil, begin by chanting *om* or any other word that is sacred to you.
Om is said to be the sound from which the universe was created. When you chant *om*, you start
by allowing your voice to resonate with a long "o" for a few moments, then change to the syllable
"um," holding the note for as long as possible. When we chant, our bodies resonate with the sound
of our voices, which changes our energy patterns. If you are feeling particularly depressed, sing
the word *love* continuously for a few minutes and notice how much better you feel.

After chanting for a few moments, ask for Israfil's help. You can even sing your request.

Israfil is the beautiful angel who brings us the music of the celestial spheres and blows the trumpet on Judgment Day. Arabic lore says Israfil spent three years with Muhammad and initiated him as a prophet. His name refers to the burning one because he assists people in burning off their limiting thoughts and the result of their old behaviors. Israfil so deeply loves all people that his tears of grief at our needless suffering would have flooded the Earth if Allah had not stopped them.

Israfil encourages us to sing and write songs. His angelic voice enfolds the listener in love, regenerating the body, mind, and soul. He inspires people to sing and to lift their spirits. Israfil will fill your heart with a deep sense of gratitude and help you see what a miracle it is to have received the gift of life. He will show you how to fill your days with beauty.

Hasmal

Associated Faith

Judaism

Hasmal will help you

- Clear up any painful communications
- Connect with your divine purpose
- Find the perfect name for a child or a pet
- Bring order to a messy house
- Balance your checkbook

Invocation

Hasmal's favorite color is deep indigo. If you want to feel his presence in your life, get some glow-in-the-dark stars and stick them up around your home. Put a few indigo stars in your wallet to assure yourself of always having abundance.

Light a deep purple candle and then say, "Hasmal, keeper of the ancient wisdoms, please help me to make choices that will benefit myself and all others involved. Help me to speak with the power only true love can bring, now and always. I humbly give thanks for your presence in my life. May your light shine brightly in my world."

Hasmal's name refers to primordial, ancient wisdoms. He is associated with the mysteries of the hidden celestial spheres where the individual letters of the Holy Name are lovingly hung. It is said that fire issues from his mouth when he speaks as he guards the throne of God. Whenever he is nearby, a brilliant, sacred white light is visible. His light guides spirits as they traverse the curtain of souls between life and death. His fiery breath burns away any limiting beliefs, which keep people from experiencing ultimate happiness.

Hasmal helps you find the sacred in even the most mundane activities. The fire that proceeds his words reminds you of the importance of all of your communications. He reminds human beings that once a word is spoken, it can never really be recalled, so choose your words carefully. Words spoken in anger can do irreparable damage, so he reminds all mortals to speak only in love.

Jeduthun

Associated Faith

Judaism

Jeduthun will help you

- Improve your singing
- Gain clarity during times of confusion
- Make positive changes

- Release negative thinking
- Lift depression
- Make your voice be heard

Invocation

When calling upon Jeduthun, put on your favorite music and sing along loudly. Sing about your cares and concerns and Jeduthun will surely respond with his loving support and lyrical voice. If you seek clarity, light a candle and bask in its gentle glow or imagine yourself surrounded by aquamarine, Jeduthun's favorite color. Then sit quietly and allow his calming voice to infuse you with his unconditional wisdom and love. When your mind and your heart are full of judgment, imagine his chorus singing forth gratitude until you feel your heart open and your mind relax.

Jeduthun leads a choir of angels in singing hymns of gratitude every evening. As the result of their chanting, much of the world's self-hatred is released and the world is blessed by angelic acceptance and love. He is called the "Master of Howling," and his voice soothes even the most troubled souls.

Legend has it that Jeduthun was once a mortal who was the chief musician of the temple. He served so faithfully that when he died, he was made an angel and given the same position in heaven. Often in life people are told to stop speaking the truth and to stop using their voices as catalyst of change. Jeduthun will empower you to take back your voice and to once again speak out when something is important to you.

Jeduthun has a sweet voice and is a wonderful leader. He will illuminate your path and help you avoid some of the pitfalls along the way.

Raziel

Associated Faith

Judaism

Raziel will help you

- Come up with great ideas
- Access your inner wisdom
- Materialize a new place to live or a great job

- Connect with spirit
- Release any limiting behaviors

Invocation

The easiest way to call upon Raziel is to light a yellow candle and say, "Raziel, my benefactor and guardian, please help me now. Help me to see life through your eyes and to make the right choices. Guide and direct my footsteps and open my mind and my heart to your incredible wisdom and love. I give thanks for the miracles that are about to occur."

As he draws near, your breath will quicken and you will feel a deep sense of well-being.

The angel Raziel stands between the veil that separates God from the rest of Creation so that he is connected to everyone and everything. A beautiful yellow aura emanates from his tall form. He has large, light blue wings and wears a robe of a magical gray material that looks like swirling liquid. Raziel is the patron of secret wisdom and divine knowledge, and the guardian of originality and pure thought.

Raziel is said to be the author of *The Book of the Angel Raziel*, which claims to contain all the mysteries of the universe. The book was likely written in the Middle Ages, but legend says that Raziel gave the book to Adam in the Garden of Eden before he was banished. Because of his care and concern for Adam, Raziel is considered a special patron of human beings. He is a messenger of the celestial realms.

Raziel will show you how to tap into the natural ebb and flow of the universe so you can manifest your deepest desires and harness the magic that lives within each human being.

Hadraniel

Hadraniel will help you

- Enrich a relationship
- Spice up your sex life
- Learn to love yourself unconditionally
- Remember the secrets of success

Invocation

When you want to call upon Hadraniel, face east and take a long, slow, deep breath. Light an icy blue-white candle and explain your wants, needs, and desires. He often signals his presence by creating a warm sensation, which will gently flow through your body. Simply ask for his guidance and allow the magic to begin.

Hadraniel's name means "majesty of God." He is a gatekeeper of heaven and one of the angels appointed as a guardian of the east wind. His mission is to awaken our knowledge of unconditional and eternal love.

He is one of the tallest angels. When he delivers God's messages, lightning flashes from his mouth. In one story, when Moses arrived in heaven to receive the Torah, Hadraniel didn't think he should have it. He made Moses weep in fear until God reprimanded Hadraniel. Then he became Moses's guide and protector. Hadraniel is also said to have given Adam the *Book of Raziel*, which contains secrets of the universe unknown even to most of the angels.

Just as lightning ionizes the air, creating that wonderful fresh smell, calling upon Hadraniel will bring a breath of fresh air into all areas of your life. Open your heart to his unconditional love. Ask for the ability to see any situation in your life through his eyes and be ready for a totally new and expansive perspective. When you see life through the eyes of love, the choices you make are bound to create happiness, joy, and ease. Judgment becomes a thing of the past, and the people and situations you attract will be much more supportive.

Pathiel

Associated Faiths

Judaism / New Age

Pathiel will help you

- Open the gates of abundance
- Overcome stupidity
- Find lost objects
- Understand assembly directions
- Straighten out computer glitches
- Follow directions
- Take exams

Invocation

Pathiel's favorite color is yellow. Ask for his assistance by writing your requests on a yellow legal pad or lighting a yellow candle. He loves to help people, so just ask for his favor. Imagine your answers easily flowing out of a beautiful cornucopia. With Pathiel's help, you can create a Manifestation Altar. Buy a cornucopia at a local craft store and place it someplace it won't be disturbed. Decorate it with flowers and words like *freedom*, *happiness*, *joy*, *abundance*, and *ease*. Include any symbols you like. Write your requests on slips of paper, place them in the cornucopia, and call upon Pathiel. Know your prayers will be answered.

Pathiel's name means "the opener." He can open a person's heart, the gates of heaven, the cornucopia of blessing, or the doorway to hell. He is very useful when evoked against forgetting and stupidity. Since Pathiel helps overcome stupidity, imagine what would happen if everyone took a few minutes each day to ask him to work with our world's leaders.

Pathiel will elevate even the most mundane goals to a spiritual level. He can enhance your creativity and bring divine inspiration to every aspect of life. Call upon him when you want things to go more smoothly. When you are having troubles with your computer or have to assemble something, Pathiel can make the whole process a lot easier.

What are your deepest dreams and desires? Pathiel will help you manifest them. Never think that any of your dreams are stupid; you wouldn't have them if you weren't able to make them come true.

Part II

Saints

Becoming a saint is quite a long and arduous process. The process of becoming a saint is called canonization. According to the Catholic Church, the Pope does not make someone a saint. A person being designated a saint only recognizes what God has already done. It can take decades or even centuries for a person to become a saint. First the local bishop must investigate the person's life. If he or she is deemed worthy, the next step toward sainthood is beatification. In order to be beatified, a candidate must be responsible for at least one posthumous miracle. After beatification, the saint must be responsible for at least one more miracle.

The lives of saints are fascinating. Some saints are able to levitate; others can be in two places at the same time (called bilocation). Some have the ability to heal others, while some are able to turn water into wine. Their ability to heal and perform miracles continues long after their deaths. During their lives, they spent a great deal of time in meditation and prayer. They developed a profound connection to their divinity. Their spiritual connection helped them realize that being of service is a wonderful way to share the unconditional love they found. Saints are always willing to help when asked for assistance.

Saints are a wonderful reminder of what is possible. If they could learn to levitate and bilocate, so can you. Saints are normal human beings who took the time to develop a deep and profound connection to God. Due to that connection, they were able to perform miracles.

What miracles would you like them to help you create in your life?

Brother André (1845–1937)

Brother André will help you

- Heal any emotional or physical ailment
- Accomplish any task
- Actualize your dreams
- Deepen your faith

Invocation

Brother André knew the power of starting small. He held a vision that he steadily moved towards manifesting. Regardless of what you want to accomplish, André's message is to take action, no matter how insignificant that action may seem.

Light a small candle and say: "Brother André, please help. May your love of Saint Joseph inspire and guide me in achieving my vision. Show me what to do and give me the strength to do it. I give thanks."

Brother André was born Alfred Bessette. Frail from birth, he suffered from chronic stomach problems that made him unable to eat solid food. At the age of twenty-five, he went to the Holy Cross Brothers seeking to become a novitiate. He was unable to read or write, but he had a note from his pastor saying, "I am sending you a saint." Alfred was deeply devoted to God and to Saint Joseph. He took the name of André.

The Holy Cross Brothers soon found that although André wanted to work, he was not strong enough, so they asked him to leave. He appealed to a visiting bishop, who agreed to let him stay until he took his vows. After he completed his training, he was sent to Notre Dame College in Montreal, where his duties included opening the door and welcoming guests.

Because of his devotion to Saint Joseph, André asked the archbishop for permission to build a chapel to Joseph on a mountain near the college. The archbishop agreed if no debt was incurred. Over the next twenty-three years, André built a series of chapels. André became an incredible healer and was known as the "Wonder Man of Mount Royal." He credited Saint Joseph for his ability to heal people. Numerous miraculous healings have been reported in Saint Joseph's oratory where André is buried.

Nicholas (died ca. 343)

Saint Nicholas will help you

- Create a perfect wedding
- In the kitchen when you bake
- Keep children safe and protected

- Travel safely
- Open your heart

Invocation

Saint Nicholas is a generous, kind-hearted soul who will help anyone in need. He has long been associated with pine trees and the color green. When you would like his assistance, light a green candle and perhaps sprinkle some pine oil. Ask for his help and then open your heart. Don't be surprised if he suggests that you give in order to receive.

Nicholas was born in Lycia, a province of Asia Minor (Turkey). As a young boy, he made pilgrimages to Egypt and Palestine. Eventually, Nicholas became the Bishop of Myra. When the Roman Emperor Diocletian imprisoned all Christians, Nicholas was exiled and put in prison. He was released in 324 when Constantine the Great became Emperor.

Nicholas was known for his generous spirit, piety, and miracles. The many stories and legends about Saint Nicholas explain why he is so well loved and why he is seen as the protector and savior of all those in need. One story tells of a poor man with three daughters. Without a proper dowry, these women would be unable to find a good husband and would surely have been sold into slavery. On three different occasions, bags of gold were thrown into their house through an open window. In some versions of the tale, the gold fell into stockings left by the fire to dry. This led to the custom of children hanging stockings to be filled with gifts by Saint Nicholas. Eventually he became associated with Father Christmas.

After his death, Nicholas was buried in Myra. His bones began to continuously ooze a sweet-smelling oil. This oil has stopped flowing only four times: when his successor was expelled from office, when his relics were moved, during World War I, and in the 1950s when the basilica was being restored.

Christopher (unknown–ca. 251)

Saint Christopher will help you

- Avoid accidents and mortal danger
- Stay safe while traveling
- Stop having nightmares
- Remain safe from sudden death and the plague

Invocation

Traditionally, people have carried a Saint Christopher medal. You can say a simple prayer, such as, "Saint Christopher, please protect me." He hears all prayers and answers with his loving touch. You will feel a sense of release as soon as you call his name.

Saint Christopher's name means "Christ carrier." There are several variations of the legend about Christopher. He is described as a tall, lean, middle-aged man with a beard. He carried a staff and lived as a hermit on the bank of a violent river. One day, a small child awoke Christopher and asked to be carried to the other side of the river. As Christopher carried the child across the river, the child got heavier and heavier until Christopher feared for his own life. Finally, he asked the child why he was so heavy. The child replied that he was the Christ child, and he was heavy with the weight of the sin in the world. On the other side, Christ told Christopher to put his staff in the ground and he would be rewarded with flowers and fruit. The next day, his staff had become a beautiful tree.

After this, Christopher went to Turkey, where he preached and converted thousands of men. The king was enraged when the knights he'd sent to capture Christopher were instead converted by him. The king then imprisoned Christopher, but Christopher remained unharmed. So the king had forty archers shoot him, but their arrows stopped in midair. One arrow turned and blinded the king. Christopher told the king his sight would be restored if he washed his eye with Christopher's blood after his death. The king had Christopher beheaded, washed his eye with the blood, and regained his sight. From this miracle came the belief that if you look at an image of Saint Christopher, you will be safe from harm. The Catholic Church renounced Christopher's status as a saint, but he is still loved by the people.

Agnes of Assisi (1197–1253)

Saint Agnes will help you

- See with greater clarity—physically and spiritually
- Become a vegetarian
- Heal a broken heart
- Connect with your spirit
- Experience a miracle

Invocation

One way to ask Agnes for help is to light a rose-scented pink candle.
Then take a few long, slow, deep breaths to center yourself. Move into the
silence of your heart and call upon her. Sit in silence until you feel her presence.
Remember that Saint Agnes is an amazing miracle worker.

Agnes was the wealthy and beloved daughter of a count. Deeply inspired by Francis of Assisi, Agnes followed her older sister, Claire, into the Saint Angelo monastery. Her father was furious about losing another daughter to the church, so he sent his brother with a group of other relatives to retrieve her. When Agnes' uncle attempted to strike her with his sword, his arm became useless. When the others with him tried to drag her out of the monastery, she was so heavy she couldn't be moved. Finally, her family realized she was protected by God, and she and Claire were allowed to stay. Saint Francis himself cut her hair because he was so impressed with her faith. Agnes' incredible faith and profound love of God will inspire you to do greatness in your own life.

When Agnes prayed, it was reported that her face would become radiant and glowing. In the monastery, Agnes and Claire went without shoes, refrained from eating meat, took no money, and maintained a contemplative silence.

Agnes eventually became the abbess. She was loved by everyone for her kind heart, generous spirit, and respectful manner. Agnes worked with the poor and established several communities dedicated to service. Numerous miracles have been reported at her tomb. Agnes is often seen surrounded by a golden light, and the scent of roses is detected in her presence.

Margaret of Antioch (died 304)

Saint Margaret will help you

- Prevent premature death
- Enhance your fertility
- Ease childbirth
- Heal kidney disease
- Bring justice to people falsely accused

Invocation

Saint Margaret is closely associated with the Virgin Mary. When you call upon her, you will often smell roses. To ask for her assistance, close your eyes and imagine yourself sitting in a beautiful garden talking with her. She will always help you if you are sincere about your request.

Saint Margaret was extremely popular during the Middle Ages. Her father was a famous pagan priest. Her mother died shortly after her birth, and Margaret was raised by her nurse, a pious Christian woman. When she embraced Christianity, her father disowned her and she was adopted by her nurse.

One day while she was in the pasture caring for a flock, she was noticed by the Roman prefect Olybrius, who wanted her as his concubine or wife. She refused his advances, so he put her on trial in Antioch. Olybrius threatened Margaret, saying that if she didn't renounce her faith, she would be tortured and killed. She refused. They tried to burn her, but the flames had no effect on her body. Then they bound her hands and feet and threw her into a pot of boiling water. As Margaret prayed, her bonds loosened and she stood up unharmed. Finally, the prefect had her beheaded. Her prayers and the peace she exhibited in the face of her trials touched the crowd deeply. She is known as a miracle worker. Her faith and love will touch your heart, mind, and soul.

Alexis (born ca. 380)

Saint Alexis will help you

- Find resources if you are homeless
- Succeed on spiritual quests
- Arrive safely and with ease when traveling

- Stay protected against earthquakes, lightning, and storms

Invocation

Saint Alexis will help anyone who humbly asks for his assistance. Humility is the key to working with Alexis. He will show you how to open your heart so you are really willing to accept help and vulnerable enough to receive the love.

Alexis was a confessor in life. He is a wonderful listener, so pour out your heart to him. When you tell him your problems, he will help you find solutions. Just be open to the suggestions even if they seem a bit unusual.

Alexis lived to be 100 years old. He was a mystic known as "the man of God." His name means "helper" or "defender." Alexis married but didn't consummate their union because Saint Paul came to him in a vision. He asked him to be of service and dedicate his life to God. His wife released him from his vows and he moved to Edessa, where he lived in a shack adjoining a church for seventeen years. He was a very pious and humble man who lived as a beggar and shared his meager resources with the poor. He liked living in anonymity.

One day the statue of the Virgin Mary told people to look for "the man of god," so in an attempt to remain anonymous he tried to flee to the city of Tarsus. A storm stopped him and he went to Rome instead, where he lived under the stairs in his family's villa until he died. His devotion and love of God continues to touch people's lives with his miraculous cures.

Kateri Tekakwitha (1656–1680)

Saint Kateri Tekakwitha will help you

- Tend your garden
- Protect the environment
- Find the perfect car
- Decorate your home

Invocation

Kateri Tekakwitha's favorite flower was the lily of the valley. If you can find a bunch of them, put them in a beautiful vase and call her name. She is a gentle soul, filled with tenderness and joy. When you ask for her help, you might feel a gentle breeze or hear a bird singing joyously.

Kateri Tekakwitha was known as the "Lily of the Mohawks." She was born in upstate New York. Her father was a Mohawk chief, and her mother was an Algonquin who had a profound faith in the Catholic religion. When she was four, smallpox attacked her village, killing her parents and her baby brother. She was left severely weakened, badly scarred, and partially blind. The light of the sun would blind her damaged eyes, so she would feel her way around. People named her Tekakwitha, which means "The One Who Walks Groping for Her Way." More poetically, her name is occasionally translated as "The One Who Puts Everything in Order." It is said that God left her in darkness to see His light.

She loved nature and often spent time simply listening to the birds and feeling the wind upon her face. Her whole countenance brightened when she was out in nature, and she helped people feel the love of the divine by seeing the beauty in the world around them.

Father Pierre Cholenec was a witness at her deathbed. He states that Kateri's face, "…so disfigured and dark in life, suddenly changed about fifteen minutes after her death, and in an instant became so beautiful and so fair that just as soon as I saw it (I was praying by her side), I let out a yell, I was so astonished, and I sent for the priest who was working at the repository for the Holy Thursday service." He too was amazed by her transformation.

She is a patron of the environment and nature. She loved the land and continues to help protect it. Kateri knows that the Earth is our gracious host and that we must take care of it.

Bernadette (1844–1879)

Saint Bernadette will help you

- Find forgiveness
- Overcome obstacles
- Conceive a child
- Heal emotionally, spiritually, and physically
- Connect with your divinity

Invocation

When you call upon Bernadette, she will take your requests directly to the Virgin Mary. A wonderful way to ask for her assistance is to sprinkle some rose petals in a beautiful bowl of water. Write your request on a piece of paper and place it under the bowl. You will often smell roses when Bernadette is present.

Mary Bernarde Soubirous was born in Lourdes, France. A sickly child, she suffered from asthma. Bernadette was a poor student and had trouble learning the catechism because she spoke a dialect of French. At fourteen, as she was gathering firewood, she came to a natural grotto where she experienced the first of eighteen visions. She saw a brilliant white light and then a small woman invited her to pray with her. Bernadette took out her rosary, and they prayed together in Bernadette's dialect. The woman instructed her to come back every day for fifteen days. Bernadette said the woman wore a white veil and a blue sash. She had a golden rose on each foot and held a long rosary.

The woman gave Bernadette personal messages and messages for the world. During these visions, Bernadette experienced trances that lasted more than an hour. The Virgin Mary didn't identify herself until the seventeenth vision. On February 25, 1858, Bernadette was instructed to drink from a spring. She began to dig. To the onlookers, it appeared she was eating dirt. The next day, in that spot, a spring began to flow. This spring has been the site of countless healings and miraculous cures.

Lourdes became one of the most beloved pilgrimage sites in the world. The spring still flows freely, and millions of miracles are attributed to its waters. The Catholic Church keeps track of the healings and periodically publishes the most noteworthy ones.

Padre Pio (1887–1968)

Padre Pio will help you

- Heal from any type of wound or disease
- Have strong relationships
- Connect with loved ones—dead and alive

- Deepen your spiritual connection
- Forgive
- Feel the presence of angels and guides
- Make wise decisions and develop your discernment

Invocation

Padre Pio was a man of great faith, so when you wish to gain his assistance, place a rose at the base of a simple cross and expect great miracles to occur in your life. Any request made with an open heart and a willingness to embrace forgiveness is sure to be graciously answered. He excels at helping you see the true nature of your challenges. He is a miracle worker, so call upon him often.

From an early age, Francesco Forgione desired to become a priest because of his deep faith in God. He prayed ceaselessly, and in 1910, his prayers were answered when he became a priest. Padre Pio was in poor health most of his childhood and suffered from tuberculosis for many years. In 1918, while praying and giving thanks before a large crucifix, the marks of the stigmata, the wounds of Christ, appeared on his body. He was cured of tuberculosis but carried the wounds of stigmata for the rest of his life. His wounds were said to give off the scent of roses.

Padre Pio had many extraordinary spiritual gifts, including the ability to heal, to bilocate, to prophecy, to perform miracles, to levitate, to see angelic beings, and to discern spirits. He was able to go without sleep and nour-

ishment; he could speak and understand languages he had never studied; and he could multiply food and drink. He was known to appear in confessionals all over the world, his invisible presence marked by the fragrance of roses. He taught people to explore the underlying cause of their problems and then asked them to forgive themselves and others. Miraculous healings took place each time a person opened his or her heart to forgiveness. As a young priest, Pope John Paul traveled a great distance to have Padre Pio hear his confession.

Padre Pio died in 1968. He had often promised that "After my death, I will do more. My real mission will begin after my death." The marks of stigmata disappeared immediately after his death.

Francis of Assisi (1181–1226)

Saint Francis will help you

- Heal animals
- Fill your heart with gratitude and love

- Find and follow your bliss
- Protect your home
- Feel God's presence in everything

Francis was the son of a rich cloth merchant. He had a good education, but he spent his early years drinking and spending his father's money. When war broke out between Assisi and neighboring Perugia, Francis was captured and thrown into jail. After he was released, he decided to join the Crusades. But then he received a visitation from Jesus, who asked Francis to serve Christ rather than the army. So Francis returned home.

He renounced his wealth, wore rough cloth, begged for food, and served the poor. Francis was known for his life with the animals he lovingly cared for and healed. He preached purity and peace and believed that all people were his brothers and sisters. Francis visited hospitals, washed lepers, and treated the sick. He also worked as a carpenter in rebuilding churches. In 1209, with the blessing of the pope, he started the Franciscan Order.

In 1224, he began to exhibit signs of the stigmata. While praying and fasting, he became so focused on the crucifixion that he went into a trance. When he awoke, he found he had nail marks on his hands and feet and a wound in his side. He kept the stigmata secret until his death.

He was known to multiply food and to influence the weather. Francis was never ordained because he didn't think he was worthy, yet he had a profound impact on the church. The gospel of kindness and love that Francis embodied soon spread all over Europe.

The Prayer of Saint Francis:
"O Lord, make me an instrument of Thy Peace!
Where there is hatred, let me sow love;
Where there is injury, pardon;
Where there is discord, harmony;
Where there is doubt, faith;
Where there is despair, hope;
Where there is darkness, light, and
Where there is sorrow, joy.
Oh Divine Master, grant that I may not
so much seek to be consoled as to console;
to be understood as to understand; to be loved
as to love; for it is in giving that we receive;
It is in pardoning that we are pardoned;
and it is in dying that we are born to Eternal Life."

Anna

Saint Anna will help you

- Heal relationships and physical ailments
- Make decisions and choices
- Feel loved and supported
- Conceive or adopt a child
- Alleviate stress

Invocation

Like her daughter Mary, Anna's symbol is the rose. When you want Anna's assistance, light a pink or red candle and ask for her help. You will often smell roses when she is near, and you may see flashes of red or pink.

Saint Anna is the mother of Mary and the grandmother of Jesus. For many years, she was unable to conceive and often went into her garden to pray for a child. Her husband, Joachim, upset about his wife's inability to have a child, went to live in a shepherd's hut, where he prayed and meditated. While he was gone, an angel came to Anna and told her she was going to have a child. She was so overjoyed that she promised the angel she would consecrate the child to be of service to God. Anna was an extremely loving mother and was well known as a healer and miracle worker. She is a great prophet and a loving guide. Saint Anna lived until she was 79 years old. In Hebrew, her name is Hanna.

In 1650, a group of sailors were caught in a violent storm off the coast of Quebec. They prayed to Saint Anna and promised to build a sanctuary for her if they survived. The ship remained afloat and the sailors all lived, so they built a shrine in her honor at Beaupre. The shrine attracts millions of people each year and is famous for the many pairs of crutches left behind by people who no longer need them.

Anna is a very beautiful and graceful woman who speaks with a lyrical voice. Her laughter will touch your heart. When you call upon her, you will feel her love immediately surround you. Anna can see into the future and will help you make decisions to enrich your life and the lives of those around you.

Gregory the Wonder-Worker

(213–270)

Gregory will help you

- Peacefully settle disputes
- Remain safe in earthquakes
- Avoid floods
- Look into the future so you can make beneficial choices
- Follow your dreams

Invocation

Gregory grew up a pagan, so he loved nature, ritual, and ceremony.
Find a quiet place in nature and ask for his assistance. You can perform
a beautiful ritual in which you create an altar out of twigs and stones,
or you could plant a tree or some flowers. As they grow, know he is
watching over you, guiding you, and helping you manifest your dreams.

Gregory was born into a distinguished pagan family and named Theodore, which means "the gift of God." He became acquainted with Christianity when he was fourteen, following his father's death. He traveled to Beirut to study law with his brother. While in Palestine, he met the famous cleric Origen and decided to pursue theology. Origen had his students study the great philosophers, including the pagan teachers. Theodore was baptized and received the Christian name of Gregory.

Gregory returned to his hometown of Neocaesarea in 238. After spending time in solitude and silent prayer, he was elected Bishop of Neocaesarea. Then he had his first recorded vision, in which Saint John and the Virgin Mary appeared to him. They were so bright he couldn't look directly at them. Mary instructed him to record these revelations and share them with his church.

Gregory took great comfort and deep inspiration from these divine visions. Calling upon "cooperation with Spirit," Gregory banished evil spirits, altered the course of rivers, and even dried up a lake that was the cause of problems between two brothers. His ability to see the future was amazing and equal to the other prophets in the Bible. Gregory became known as the "miracle worker," and his miraculous feats and loving wisdom converted many people.

Columba (521–597)

Saint Columba will help you

- Protect against computer hackers
- Stop plagiarism
- Enhance creativity
- Inspire poetry and prose
- Remove obstacles to getting your work published

Invocation

Columba turned from his anger in order to honor people and to care for their spiritual needs. He is a gentle man who will gladly help you enhance and protect your creativity. Since he loved bards and poets, one way of connecting with him is to write a rhyme or loudly sing your request. His sense of humor will help you even if you can't carry a tune.

Columba's birth name was Crimthann, which means "the fox." Ordained before the age of twenty-five, Columba spent the next fifteen years preaching and establishing religious communities in Ireland at Derry, Durrow, and Kells. He was also said to have illicitly copied a psalter. When King Diarmait ruled that the copy had to be returned, Columba was infuriated.

Later Columba harbored a kinsman who had killed an opponent in a hurling tournament. The king ordered his men to ignore the "right of sanctuary" and kill the kinsman. Columba gathered his clan and attacked the king.

When the battle ended, the king had lost 3,000 men while Columba lost only one. He was condemned by the church and sent with twelve companions to the island of Iona, off the coast of Scotland, where he founded a monastery.

Columba became known for his miracles, including raising the dead, healing, taming wild animals, calming storms, calling rain, and turning water into wine. Columba had many visions. The patron saint of Ireland, he was so fond of Celtic history that he protected the bards and the poets who sang and wrote about it.

Ambrose

(ca. 339–397)

Saint Ambrose will help you

- Forgive
- Become a father and care for your family
- Increase your faith
- Gain financial independence

Invocation

Ambrose is a man of faith. He found great peace in his connection to God, and he will show you how to find that connection within your own heart for yourself. He will show you how to create miracles in your life and the lives of others. Ask him to embrace you with his faith and his love. Light a candle, say a prayer, and then trust the guidance you are given.

Saint Ambrose is known for his miracles and his writings. He was a lawyer and the governor of Milan. He owned a large estate and was a close friend of the emperor. It was a time of great strife in the Catholic Church. The bishop supported the Arian heresy that did not believe that Christ was a divinity. The bishop died, and there was a riot in the cathedral between the Arians and the Catholics. As governor, Ambrose was in charge of keeping public order. He went to the church and gave a passionate speech for peace. He begged people to decide their differences without violence. Suddenly there was a chant, "Ambrose for Bishop."

Ambrose hadn't even been baptized, and at first, he resisted the idea. He even filled his home with prostitutes so he would be considered unacceptable by the church and the people. Ambrose tried to hide, but Emperor Valentitian threatened severe penalties to anyone who hid him. After much inner turmoil, he became the bishop. He gave away all his wealth, prayed often, and fasted regularly. He studied the Greek philosophers and read the Scriptures. Ambrose became a wonderful bishop. He preached against capital punishment and was a proponent of peace. He became a mystic and a healer. He healed by laying his hands on people and is said to have raised the dead. He died on Good Friday, April 4, 397. He had a profound aura of peace around him at the time of his death. His writings, including sermons, hymns, homilies, and mystical tracts, touched many people and guided many leaders of the church for many years.

John of the Cross   (1542–1591)

Saint John will help you

- Remember that miracles are possible
- Have a mystical experience
- Embrace all of life
- See the perfection in all of creation
- Forgive yourself and others

Invocation

Saint John connected with the divine through prayer. To ask for his assistance,
say a simple prayer, describe your problem, open your heart, and ask for his help.
He is a constant reminder that anything is possible, so call upon him often.
He often works through other people, so watch for unexpected help from kind and
generous strangers. John had such a deep connection to God that simply opening
your heart to his love will open up your own connection in miraculous ways.

John was a Spanish mystic and a Renaissance poet. At the age of fourteen, he took a job in a hospital working with incurable patients and the insane. He learned to see the beauty and happiness of God in everything. His greatest love was God.

He worked with Saint Teresa to reform the Carmelite order. In retaliation for the reforms, he was put in a small cell and regularly beaten. He continued to pray and to deepen his connection with God. After nine months, he escaped by climbing out a window, taking only the poetry he had written with him. John hid in a convent and read his mystical poetry to the nuns.

For the rest of his life, John shared his experience of God's love. He wrote many books filled with practical advice on spiritual growth and prayer. He said, "Where there is no love, put love—and you will find love."

Of the many miracles that are attributed to John, perhaps the most famous was that while the monastery was being repaired, the walls of his prison cell crumbled. After the rubble was cleared, he was found standing unharmed in the corner. He said the Virgin Mary had covered him with her arms and protected him from harm. He was also seen levitating while praying. When his body was unearthed in 1955, it was still in perfect condition and smelled of roses.

Cecelia (second or third century)

Saint Cecilia will help you

- Improve your singing
- Compose music
- Succeed at any musical endeavor

- Deepen your faith
- Feel safe and loved no matter what is happening around you

Invocation

To call upon Cecelia, light a rose-scented candle and softly whisper her name. If you have an altar, place a bouquet of roses or lilies on it, write your request on paper, and place the paper next to the vase. She will surely help you.

Cecelia was born in Rome. As a young girl, she decided she wanted to remain a virgin and to dedicate her life to God. Her parents arranged a marriage for her. She told her new husband she had an angel watching over her, and if the marriage was consummated, her husband would suffer greatly, but if he agreed to be baptized, he would be allowed to see the angel. When her husband returned from being baptized, he found Cecelia praying with an angel beside her. The angel had flaming wings and wore two crowns, one of lilies and the other of roses.

The angel offered him a wish. He said he wanted his brother to be baptized. When his brother arrived, he remarked on the fragrance of the flowers, which were out of season. After Cecelia's husband told his brother about the angel and the two crowns, his brother was also baptized. They dedicated their lives to burying the martyrs who were being killed in the city every day. Both brothers were subsequently killed.

Cecilia was told to denounce her faith, but she refused. She was ordered to be killed by suffocation, but the attempt failed. Then she was beheaded, but she lived for three days, converting hundreds with her faith and her words. Her voice was so beautiful that people said she could charm the birds out of the trees. She was buried in a secret location. In 1599, her body and clothing were found intact. Her Cyprus casket was put on display and was reputed to smell faintly of roses.

Anthony of Padua (1195–1231)

Saint Anthony will help you

- Find lost objects, pets, or missing people
- Remember who you really are
- Connect with your divinity
- Ease a pregnancy
- Travel safely

Invocation

Saint Anthony has a loving heart devoted to service. Stand quietly, close your eyes, and call his name several times. Then state your request and ask for his help. You may feel a slight breeze or a sense of warmth, which signals his presence.

Anthony is usually depicted wearing brown Franciscan robes, holding a book in one hand and the baby Jesus in the other. He is a beloved saint to many Catholics and is known as the "saint of miracles." An elegant speaker, Anthony inspires profound love within the hearts of his listeners. His resonant voice reflects his deep connection with his divinity. He prayed constantly and attracted huge crowds with his ability to impact others with his words. It is said that once, when he walked along the sea, the fish rose out of the water to listen to him speak about the wonders of faith. He inspired thousands of people from the pulpit and was a champion for the poor, prisoners, the disenfranchised, and debtors. He protected his listeners from rain and was known for his miracles. It is said that he once miraculously repaired a farmer's field that had been trampled by the crowds.

After he died, he appeared to the abbot at Vercelli, who then announced his passing to the people of Padua. When his body was moved three hundred years after his death, his tongue was perfect and still red. It is believed this was due to the purity of his teachings. He is known for finding lost articles and missing persons.

A legend says that when Anthony was staying with friends, the host found him sitting in absolute ecstasy holding the baby Jesus. Anthony at times is also represented holding a lily for purity and a book for wisdom. He is often depicted with his devout mule.

Teresa of Avila   (1515–1582)

Saint Teresa will help you

- Relieve headaches
- Deepen your spiritual connection
- Prevent heart attacks
- Heal a broken heart

Invocation

When you would like to invite Saint Teresa's help, say a silent prayer. You could place a bouquet of roses next to a small white candle to symbolize her presence. Learning how to use passive mental prayer will help in all areas of your life.

Teresa was born to a wealthy family. As a teenager, she was wild and rebellious, so her father sent her to a convent when she was sixteen. At first she hated it, but eventually she chose to stay because she saw how miserable her mother had been in marriage.

Teresa felt unworthy of God's love. She hated to pray, yet she prayed a lot. Eventually she fell ill and became paralyzed. At one point, a grave was dug for her and she was given last rites. Through daily mental prayer, she was able to heal herself and be relieved of horrible pain. She attributed her healing to Saint Joseph.

Teresa began to develop a rich and rewarding relationship with God. She had visions and profound ecstasy from which she would receive inspiration. Teresa described passive mental prayer as a four-step process. The first step is easy: Just meditate. The second step is to quiet the senses so the soul can receive guidance. In the third step, you open to contact with God. There is no stress, just a mental surrender to the process. The fourth step is taken by God. You need only remain open and receptive to God's wisdom, guidance, and gifts.

People who saw Teresa in prayer said she looked as if she was in a trance. She would often awaken drenched with tears of pure joy. As with many other saints, after her death, she radiated a sweet odor and her body remained uncorrupted for many years. Her coffin was said to smell of roses.

Brigid of Ireland (born ca. 450)

Saint Brigid will help you

- Bless your home
- Deepen your ability to love
- Increase your abundance
- Conceive a child
- Heal a sick child
- Heal eye problems and hopeless wounds

Invocation

Light a yellow candle and call her name. Simply explain what you
would like her to help you with. She is a woman with a deep love for everyone,
so when you invite her into your life, expect loving miracles.

Brigid is the dearly beloved saint of Ireland. There is speculation she is actually a Celtic goddess who was made a saint in order to convert Celts to Christianity.

Born half princess and half slave, she lived with her mother, who had been sold to a Druid. From an early age, Brigid was devoted to God. After hearing Saint Patrick speak, she gave whatever she had to those in need. Brigid was a gracious woman who helped the poor with a loving and open heart.

When her mother was old and ill, Brigid took over running the dairy. She continued to give away all she could, and the Druid got upset. He tried to entrap her by asking her to bring him a basket of butter, which he knew she had already given away. Miraculously, when she handed him the basket, it was full. He was so impressed with the miracle he set her mother free. In another story, the Virgin Mary appeared to her and was upset because their conversation was interrupted by the crowds Brigid attracted. Brigid took a rake and made the tines appear to be candles. The crowd was distracted so Mary could finish the conversation.

Brigid is pictured as a beautiful young woman in a white robe. She is often shown carrying a lantern. A cross made of rushes is often associated with her. She worked closely with the poor, increasing their limited resources, healing the sick, helping worried mothers, and blessing the cradles of newborns. Brigid touches the hearts of everyone who calls upon her.

Martin of Charity (1579–1639)

Saint Martin will help you

- Find your soul mate
- Create racial harmony
- Conceive a child
- Heal any physical, emotional, or spiritual problem
- Experience a miracle
- Find a lost pet

Invocation

Light a red candle before you ask for Martin's help at night. Then take a few minutes to pray. Begin by thinking about all the things for which you are grateful. Then explain your problem and ask for his help. Close by asking his blessing for people in need around the world.

Martin was the illegitimate son of a mixed-blood free woman in Panama. He inherited his mother's dark complexion and features. His father acknowledged him when he was eight, but then abandoned him again. Martin grew up in poverty. At twelve, he was apprenticed to a barber-surgeon. He learned to cut hair, administer medicine, and bleed people, a popular medical treatment at the time.

A few years later, Martin applied to the Dominicans to become a lay helper. After nine years, the community asked that he be made a Brother. Martin prayed endlessly and took care of the sick and the poor. He treated all people, regardless of color or race, including slaves brought from Africa. He also founded an orphanage.

Martin demonstrated many miraculous gifts. He was an incredible healer who performed instantaneous cures. While in the ecstasy of prayer, he would float in midair and the room would be filled with light. He was able to bilocate (be in two places at once) and had an incredible rapport with animals.

Martin forgave the mice and rats in the kitchen, saying they were hungry. He adopted stray cats and dogs, which he kept at his sister's house. He became a fundraiser for the priory and the city. Whether he sought blankets or miracles, his prayers were always answered. Even though he became the spiritual director for hundreds of people, he always called himself a "poor slave."

Agatha (died ca. 250)

Saint Agatha will help you

- Overcome the emotional trauma of sexual assault
- Prevent fires
- Stay safe during natural disasters

- Defend torture victims
- Heal breast disease
- Find shelter during stormy weather

Invocation

Compassion is the hallmark of Saint Agatha. She will help you open your heart and find forgiveness so you can free yourself from the pain of the past. You can light a small white candle, say a simple prayer, and know she will be there for you. She will show you how you can find peace and happiness in the midst of life's traumas.

Agatha was a virgin and martyr. She was born of a wealthy family and was beautiful. The time in which she lived was a period of severe persecution for Christians, yet she refused to marry a Roman consul because she had dedicated her life to being a virgin of Christ. She was sent to a brothel but remained a virgin. Then she was accused of being a Christian and was turned over to the magistrate. She was beaten and tortured but was sustained by her love of God. The magistrate was so enraged by her cheerful continence that he had her breasts crushed and cut off. Saint Peter came to her in a vision that night and healed her wounds. Unimpressed by the miracle, the magistrate had her rolled over hot coals and broken clay pots. She prayed for release from her pain, and the earth began to tremble with a violent earthquake. She died with a look of peace on her face.

Her courage and pious love of God fostered a cult following. Prayers to her were reported to cure people of a variety of ills and to stop Mount Etna from erupting. She was credited with stopping the Turks from invading Malta. Medieval paintings of her showed her carrying a tray with her breasts, which many people thought were really loaves of bread, creating the tradition of blessing bread on feast day. Agatha's faith allowed her to feel peace in the midst of physical torture.

Patrick

(ca. 389–461)

Saint Patrick will help you

- Overcome a fear of snakes
- Improve your sense of humor
- Overcome prejudice or exclusion

- Build a life, a home, a building, or a relationship

Invocation

Light an emerald green candle and focus attention on your request. Ask Saint Patrick to show you the way and to embrace you with his wisdom and his love. Then give thanks for his help. You'll be amazed by the solutions that come to you.

Saint Patrick is one of the world's most popular saints. On his feast day, it seems like everyone is Irish! His Roman parents ruled the colony of Britain. At the age of fourteen, Patrick was captured by Irish slaver traders and taken into captivity. Ireland was a land of Druids and pagans. He learned the language and their practices.

During his captivity, Patrick turned to God in prayer. He wrote, "The love of God and his fear grew in me more and more, as did the faith, and my soul was roused, so that, in a single day, I have said as many as a hundred prayers and in the night, nearly the same. I prayed in the woods and on the mountain, even before dawn. I felt no hurt from the snow or ice or rain."

When he was twenty, he had a dream that led him to escape Ireland and return to Britain. Later, another dream urged him to return to Ireland. There Patrick became a priest and was later ordained a bishop. The shamrock is associated with him because he often used it to explain the trinity of Father, Son, and Holy Spirit.

There are many legends and miracles attributed to Patrick. Above all, he was a humble, pious, gentle man. His love and total devotion and trust in God created miracles in his life and in the lives of those around him.

Joseph   (1603–1663)

Saint Joseph will help you

- Stay safe when traveling
- Heal
- Succeed on a spiritual quest
- Find lost pets

Invocation

When you call upon Saint Joseph, look up and call his name.
Explain the nature of your request and know he will be there.
When he is present, you will smell the faint odor of sweet perfume.

Joseph became an incredible Franciscan mystic, healer, and visionary. His father, a poor carpenter, died before Joseph's birth. His mother was thrown out of her home and gave birth to Joseph in a stable. He was born with deformed feet. As a child, he was mentally slow but had a quick temper. Joseph had his first ecstatic vision when he was eight. At seventeen, he applied to become a friar but was rejected because of his sketchy education. Finally, the Franciscans accepted him as a lay brother. After working in the stables for many years, his temper cooled and he was ordained as a priest at twenty-five.

Joseph became famous for his ability to levitate. Almost anything religious would trigger his ecstatic aerial flights. He would fly high over the heads of the people and float for long periods of time. He would often fly to altars and holy statues. More than seventy of his flights were documented. Because of the huge crowds that gathered to see him fly, Joseph wasn't allowed to conduct mass and was asked to stay in his room. For the last thirty-five years of his life, he was a virtual prisoner in his room. A chapel was built for him there so he could pray privately.

Joseph was able to bilocate and was credited with many miraculous healings. He could read people's minds and see into their hearts. He could control the elements and communicate with animals. Everything Joseph touched was infused with the sweet smell of perfume.

Bridget of Sweden   (1304–1373)

Saint Bridget will help you

- Be protected against miscarriage
- Feel comfort if you have lost a loved one

- Courageously follow your heart's desire
- Work towards your life's purpose
- Interpret dreams

Invocation

Bridget was a pious woman who requires only an open heart and a sincere request. Light your favorite scented candle and take a few minutes to become quiet and focused before you call on her. Then offer a simple prayer, asking for her wisdom and guidance.

From an early age, Bridget had prophetic dreams and visions. When she was thirteen, Bridget's father arranged a marriage for her with eighteen-year-old Prince Ulf. It was a happy marriage in which she had eight children. Bridget was a pious woman devoted to her religious beliefs. At thirty-two, she was summoned to become a lady-in-waiting to the Queen of Sweden. When she arrived, she was upset by the royal lifestyle and unsuccessfully tried to influence the king and queen to change their ways.

After a number of years, she obtained a leave of absence, and she and her husband went on a pilgrimage. Her visions told her she had a mission to work for reform.

Her husband and she then separated, each of them dedicating their lives to God within separate religious orders.

Bridget became troubled by her visions, fearing they were her own imagination. At the urging of a message in a vision, she consulted Master Matthias, a canon. He said her dreams were truly from God. She then dictated her dreams and visions, which were recorded in Latin. The church was in turmoil at that time. Bridget's visions helped bring the papacy back to Rome from Avignon in southern France.

Following the messages of her dreams, Bridget founded a monastery and embarked on many pilgrimages, including one to the Holy Land.

Part III

Ascended Masters, Spirit Guides, and Master Teachers

Ascended masters are people who have become enlightened during their lives and have chosen to continue to serve humanity after their ascension as well. They have released all of their limiting beliefs and are able to see all of life through the eyes of love. They can come and go at will from the earth plane and are always willing to be of assistance to anyone who asks.

Spirit guides are spiritual beings that are willing to act as guides. They are very similar to guardian angels and are more than willing to help you if you just ask them. They will never interfere in your life unless you ask for their help. They won't do the work for you, but they will certainly give you a more expansive perspective and help you make choices that will add to the quality of your life.

Master teachers are beings that love to teach people and help them let go of their limiting beliefs. They have walked the path before you and can help you avoid some of the speed bumps and pitfalls. If you ask for directions, they will help you find the easiest and most direct route to where you want to go and what you want to create.

They are all wonderful assistants. Give yourself the opportunity to get to know them. Each of the masters has his or her own unique personality and specialties. As you become more familiar with them, you will intuitively know whom to ask for help in any circumstance.

What area of your life would you like them to light up with their wisdom, love, and light?

Enoch

(3284–3017 B.C.E.)

Enoch will help you

- Bring justice to any injustice
- Savor all of life
- Deepen your spiritual connection
- Successfully complete writing projects
- Heal problems with breathing

Invocation

Enoch is waiting for your call and delights in helping anyone who takes the time to ask for his assistance. Light a golden-colored candle and call his name. State the nature of your problem and ask for his wisdom and guidance. Pay particular attention to your dreams; because he is a master of symbols, Enoch often communicates in allegory.

There are many different versions of Enoch's role in history. Enoch was a biblical prophet who became an ascended master. He is credited with inventing the concept of books and then later writing the Book of Enoch. He lived a very pious life. As a leader of his people, he was always just and fair. His name in Hebrew signifies "initiator" or "initiated." In the Koran, he is referred to as a man of truth and a prophet.

Enoch taught extensively about the power of symbols and is said to have discovered the knowledge and power of the Zodiac. He is credited with passing down symbols from time before time that explain the great mysteries. He is the custodian of great philosophical and religious truths that remain unknown to the world at large.

He was described as being a direct descendant of Adam and the great grandfather of Noah. He lived to be 365 years old and then ascended into heaven. Enoch was said to walk frequently with God, and on one of those walks, he simply ascended. He often reminded people that they too could have profound communion with God if they just took the time to practice that connection as they did the mundane tasks in their lives.

Moses

Moses will help you

- Illuminate your way
- Understand the power of faith
- Create abundance

Invocation

Ask Moses to teach you how to live a life of faith as he did:

"Moses, show me the way of faith. Help me to feel the deep and abiding presence of love in my life. Help me to relinquish control and know peace. Show me the way, guide me, and direct me. May I have the willingness to follow that divine guidance. I give thanks."

Moses plays a huge role in the Bible and is credited with writing the first five books. He had a close and intimate relationship with God. The turning point in Moses's life was when God appeared to him in a burning bush and told him to go back to Egypt and lead his people to freedom. Moses is often called the lawgiver because he received the Ten Commandments from God on Mount Sinai.

Moses is an incredible role model and wonderful teacher about the power of faith, trusting the process, and accepting what is. He was able to perform amazing miracles because of his faith and his dependence on his profound connection to God. He shows us what is possible when we have a complete commitment and unwavering faith.

Moses led his people into the desert, where God provided manna each day. He told the people to gather what they needed each day for themselves and those who couldn't do it for themselves, but not to gather any more than they needed. Some people stored some for the next day and in the morning found it full of maggots and very smelly. Those who gathered a lot had barely enough, and those who gathered just enough had more than they needed. This is a powerful lesson anyone can apply to his or her life.

What about you? Do you sputter and spew, or do you trust the process inherently? Are you generous of spirit, or do you fear what may happen next? You may not have seen a burning bush, but Moses can help you deepen your connection to God and have faith so you move smoothly in the direction of your bliss.

Solomon

(ca. 1000 B.C.E.)

Solomon will help you

- Connect with your divine wisdom
- Balance all areas of your world
- Invite success and abundance into your life
- Heal your emotional body
- Release the past

Invocation

Solomon reminds people of the importance of the spirit of selflessness. The color he most resonates with is aqua blue. If you would like to work with Solomon, say this simple prayer: "Solomon, master of wisdom, please help me. Guide me with your brilliant light, love, and generous spirit. Show me the way so I may help others find theirs."

Solomon was best known for his wisdom. He wrote more than three thousand proverbs and one thousand songs.

Perhaps the most famous story concerns a dispute between the two women who came to his court both claiming they were the mother of the same baby. Solomon threatened to split the baby in half. One woman was prepared to accept the decision, but the other begged him to give the live baby to the other woman. Solomon then knew the second woman was the mother.

Solomon learned to balance the religious with the secular. By accessing the ancient wisdom of his spirit and channeling it through an open heart and a loving mind, he was able to bring peace and abundance to his country and build a great temple. If you ask for his help, he will show you how to do the same thing in your life.

Solomon will show you how to connect with your inner wisdom. Where do you argue for your own limitations? How do you sabotage your own success? Where do you fail to respect your own wants and needs? Do you try to please others rather than taking care of yourself? Are you too busy to take care of your spiritual, emotional, and physical needs? Do you worry about the future?

White Eagle

(mythological)

White Eagle will help you

- See your perfection
- Connect with your divinity
- Release all of your limitations
- Learn how to love unconditionally
- Heal your mind, body, and spirit

Invocation

White Eagle often worked with the symbol of the water lily. A wonderful way to begin working with him is to visualize a water lily and think of it as your spiritual unfoldment. Create a mental picture of a beautiful garden. Walk through the garden to the innermost sanctuary until you see the silent pool of still water that represents your spirit. Look into that water and see the true reflection of yourself, for the waters of the spirit never lie. Floating in the water is a pure white lily with a center of gold, symbolic of purity and divine intelligence. And as you look at that flower, know the light of your spirit is transforming your entire life to reflect your true perfection.

White Eagle's message is a familiar one. He knows that the only limitations that exist are the ones we place upon ourselves. He works in a very simple and profound manner reminding you that as you develop your true nature, your spiritual light will radiate out into your life, blessing, healing, and transforming your world. Letting your spiritual light radiate is like having a pair of wings. That light sets you free and allows you to soar.

He sees only the spiritual perfection in everyone and everything. Without that spiritual light, nothing exists. White Eagle will show you how to expand that connection so you can manifest whatever you want when you want it.

He reminds you that you already know how to manifest and will help you let go of the limiting thoughts you have that cause you to manifest what you don't want.

White Eagle will help you heal your life and see your reality in a totally new light, one that is free of fear. His love will enfold you and make releasing your fear a fun and playful exercise. His joy is infectious; he is a beautiful spirit filled with love and laughter. White Eagle's healing begins with the simple and profound exercise of radiating the light of pure spirit throughout your entire being. By radiating this perfect light, you will be filled with a sense of comfort, joy, and strength.

Muhammad (ca. 570–632)

Muhammad will help you

- Open your heart to divine love
- Meditate
- Deepen your ability to savor life
- See the divine in all of life

Invocation

Muhammad is a loving man of profound faith. He will show you how
to create a profound and life-changing connection with the divine
for yourself, if you ask with an open heart and a willing mind.

Muhammad is the prophet attributed with transcribing the Koran, the basic text of Islam, from the angel Gabriel. He led a simple life and was known for honesty and integrity. He was a man of his word and had a great deal of love and compassion for humans and animals alike. Muhammad was twenty-five years old when he married Khadija, a rich widow of Mecca, who was forty years old. She was a gentle, loving woman of impeccable character.

Muhammad was in the habit of going to a cave in the desert three miles from Mecca, spending months in prayer and meditation. After his visitation from Gabriel, Muhammad experienced a profound connection with the divine. Muhammad spoke publicly about his conversion and converted many by the sincerity and love in his words.

Muhammad served everyone, especially those in need, such as widows, orphans, the poor, sick, aged, and homeless. He set many slaves free and ministered to sick animals. He milked cows and fed camels. He never felt he was better than anyone else, and he was always willing to be of service. Above all else, he was a man of peace. One of Islam's basic tenants is that there is one god, Allah, and it encourages a simple life based on love and respect for the creator and for all of creation.

In one of the stories about Muhammad, he was in the desert, where some simple men were praying. A pious man asked them which direction they faced when they prayed. Muhammad admonished him by saying, "This poor shepherd's simple prayer entered directly into the ears of Allah more clearly than yours, as it was uttered from his heart with intense love, faith, sincerity, and reverence."

Confucius

(551–479 B.C.E.)

Confucius will help you

- Make a decision
- Overcome a moral dilemma
- Illuminate legal issues
- Increase your profit margin
- Enhance your love life

Invocation

Confucius was a simple man who loved helping people live life to its fullest.
A wonderful way to call upon him is to sit down with a cup of green tea, relax,
take a few long breaths, and explain the nature of your problem. Then ask of his
wisdom and guidance. Be observant for the next few days. His assistance may show
up in a variety of ways. You may notice a billboard or a headline in a newspaper or
may feel called to read a certain book. Rest assured he will come to your aid.

Confucius was born in the Lu province of China with the birth name of K'ung Ch'iu. His father died when he was three. Confucius helped support his mother while managing to obtain an excellent education in music, poetry, history, and sports. After his mother's death, he became a teacher of the six disciplines: poetry, music, history, government, etiquette, and divination. He became chief justice and then received a prestigious position that allowed him to spend the rest of his life compiling his writings.

Confucius was a thinker, an educator, a political figure, and a philosopher. He became famous for his eloquent sayings about nature and the world. The essence of Confucianism is striving for perfect virtue in every thought, word, and deed. Confucius had a simple moral code: love others, do what is right rather than what is easiest or most profitable, and treat others as you wish to be treated. He believed a ruler who had to resort to force had already failed as a leader.

Some quotes attributed to Confucius:
- "And remember, no matter where you go, there you are."
- "Better a diamond with a flaw than a pebble without."
- "Choose a job you love, and you will never have to work a day in your life."

Paul the Venetian (ascended 1588)

Paul the Venetian will help you

- Learn about divine love and true compassion
- Enhance your creativity
- Put love in motion in your life
- Succeed in your chosen field of art, architecture, or engineering
- Deepen your connection to your spirit

Invocation

Paul loves beauty, so when you call upon him, surround yourself in beauty. Cover a table with a vividly colored cloth and arrange some flowers and candles on it. Light the candles and call his name. He is a creative master, so his suggestions may be unusual. After you ask for his help, grab some colored pens and draw. See what images appear and look for symbolism. Write yourself a love letter and read it every day. Take daily concrete actions that say I love you. Volunteer at a homeless shelter or work with animals. Make love an activity in your life that you practice each and every day.

During his last incarnation, Paul lived as an artist. He saw beauty as the most powerful agent of change in a person's life. He painted in vivid colors and developed a way to prepare paint that allowed the color to last for centuries. He was summoned before the tribunal of the Inquisition because of his creative interpretation of the Last Supper in which he included a dwarf, a parrot, dogs, and a jester.

Paul the Venetian teaches about divine love, compassion, and charity. Creativity and beauty are other important qualities he emphasizes. Paul believes divine love is really love in action. He suggests moving from contemplated love into expressing love by the actions one takes.

It is through deeds that love is most visible. He will help you define and clarify your concepts about divine love. He explains that true compassion lifts up another's soul, while human sympathy allows the person to wallow without progressing on the spiritual path.

Paul applauds our innate beauty as a magnificent creation of God, and he champions the pursuit of our Higher Self. The Ascended Master Paul the Venetian helps people master using love as a creative force in their lives. He also works closely with students of art, music, architecture, and engineering to help them create beauty, symmetry, and design.

Hilarion (fourth century)

Hilarion will help you

- Unsnarl your computer
- Write music
- Connect with your deepest inner truths

- Open your ability to heal
- Connect with and teach spiritual truths

Invocation

Hilarion is a miracle worker, so call on him frequently. Write his name on the bottom of a forest green candle and light it every day as you meditate. Ask for his guidance and assistance. Invite him to help you open up to the blessings of the Holy Spirit.

Breathe in love and breathe out anything unlike love. Imagine Hilarion reaching out and touching your head and your heart. Be open to his presence in your life and find ways to be of service to others. He will work magic in your mind, heart, and spirit.

Hilarion was born in Palestine in the fourth century. He lived as a hermit and was well known for his countless miracles. His ability to cure the sick and to bring much-needed rain attracted many followers. He tried to find seclusion by moving continuously, but crowds continued to seek him out. They followed him even into the most remote regions. Eventually, he realized that his gifts of healing and truth-telling were meant to be shared, not hidden.

As an ascended master, Hilarion works closely with spiritual teachers, people interested in the healing arts, scientists, engineers, musicians, and computer scientists. Hilarion was a high priest at the Temple of Truth in Atlantis and also worked with the Oracle of Delphi. He helps people develop discernment, so they can tell the difference between the truth and illusion.

Hilarion assists people in preparing to fully connect with the Holy Spirit and to manifest their gifts of healing. Perhaps his greatest gift is his ability to help you open your heart while quieting your doubt-filled mind.

Sri Swami Satchidananda (1914–2002)

Sri Swami Satchidananda will help you

- Remember that everything in life is a gift
- Joyfully embrace all of you
- Be truly happy

- Expand your capacity to meditate so you can connect more deeply
- Know you are one with everything

Invocation

Just ask and Sri Swami Satchidananda will gladly help you. Practice smiling with your heart when you ask for his assistance. He will bring a sense of magic, wonder, and joy into your life. You will feel his love surround you, and a sense of ease will become evident in everything that you do.

"Your ultimate goal is to be happy. Where is that happiness? Within you. If you want to have permanent happiness, it will never come from outside. If somebody makes you happy today, the same person will make you unhappy tomorrow. You are happiness and peace personified. Find that happiness and peace within you."

—*His Holiness Sri Swami Satchidananda*

Sri Swami Satchidananda loves people and loves helping them. He absolutely loves reminding people about the joy that surrounds everything and is always available. He is the personification of love and joy. When you call upon him, you are likely to hear joyful laughter and feel like smiling. He is a deeply spiritual being, and his desire for everyone is to experience the incredible feeling created by a sense of connection to one's divinity. He has a very simple philosophy, and his guidance is always very gentle, loving, and transformative. Sri Swami Satchidananda saw the similarity in all of the world's religions and knew that we are all part of the great whole.

When asked how he always stayed happy, he replied, "You want my secret? I never worry. Whatever comes, comes, and I accept it fully as the gift of God." He sees everything as a gift and felt that having a physical body was nothing short of a miracle. He will help you realize that life is a vehicle you can use to savor each moment and remember who and what you really are.

Lady of Guadalupe (appeared 1531)

Lady of Guadalupe will help you

- Conceive a child
- Heal a broken heart
- Strengthen all of your relationships
- Find the love of your life

Invocation

Lady of Guadalupe is more than willing to help you. Place some cut roses in a vase and scatter some rose petals around your room. Light a candle and ask her for her assistance. Pour out your heart to her and listen for her guidance. She will embrace you with her love. When you share that love, it comes back to you multiplied.

In 1531, Juan Diego, who had recently become a Catholic, was walking to his religious instruction in a small town in Mexico. Suddenly he heard birds singing, and he wondered where he was. Then he heard a lyrical voice calling his name. He was puzzled and when he looked around, he saw a beautiful woman standing a few feet away. She told him to talk to the bishop and have a church built in that spot for her. The bishop wouldn't believe Juan at first, but she kept encouraging him to talk to the bishop. Finally she had him pick flowers that were blooming in the middle of the desert in the middle of the winter. He filled his jacket with the flowers. When he opened his jacket to give them to the bishop, there was an image of the heavenly lady clearly imprinted on the inside.

Our Lady of Guadalupe is well known for her miracles. Her image on Juan's jacket is the only physical manifestation of the Virgin Mary. She is a powerful force of love and teaches about the power of faith, hope, and charity. Lady of Guadalupe is the embodiment of divine love. She is the divine mother who cares deeply for all of her children. She will never judge you and is always ready to help. Lady of Guadalupe is a compassionate guide who will teach you how to fill your life with laughter and joy.

Mother Teresa   (1910–1997)

Mother Teresa will help you

- Find your life's purpose
- Overcome grief
- Heal a broken heart
- Comfort a child

Invocation

Mother Teresa loves to be of service, so feel free to call upon her. She was a simple woman, so you don't have to do anything fancy. Light a white candle and call her name. Explain what you would like her to help you with and ask for her assistance. Open your heart, and spend some time in silence so you can hear her suggestions.

Mother Teresa was awarded the Nobel Peace Prize, and she spent more than forty-five years comforting the poor, the dying, and the unwanted around the world. Her love transcended death, and she continues to work with people, teaching them about the power of love, faith, gratitude, and being of service. As a young woman, she found a dying woman on the streets of Calcutta. She stayed with her, comforting her until she died. That experience changed her life, and she made it her calling to help those in need.

It is said she had this prayer on her wall, and it nicely sums up her philosophy:

"People are often unreasonable, irrational, and self-centered. Forgive them anyway.

If you are kind, people may accuse you of selfish, ulterior motives. Be kind anyway.

If you are successful, you will win some unfaithful friends and some genuine enemies. Succeed anyway.

If you are honest and sincere, people may deceive you. Be honest and sincere anyway.

What you spend years creating, others could destroy overnight. Create anyway.

If you find serenity and happiness, some may be jealous. Be happy anyway.

The good you do today will often be forgotten. Do good anyway.

Give the best you have, and it will never be enough. Give your best anyway.

In the final analysis, it is between you and God. It was never between you and them anyway."

Elijah

Elijah will help you

- Deepen your faith
- Tune in to your inner wisdom
- Remember that miracles are possible when you believe

Invocation

Allow yourself to relax when you call upon Elijah. He was a man of peace, so taking time to quiet your mind will help you connect with him. Take a few long, slow, deep breaths and let go. Relax and open your heart. Spend a few minutes breathing deeply and connecting with the solitude of your heart. After a few minutes, you will feel that connection, and then ask Elijah for his help. Call his name out loud. Allow him to show you how to connect with your inner wisdom. He has a generous heart and is always willing to help you. He will remind you that you connect with the divine through the silence of your mind. Whenever you want his help, just call his name out loud and he will be there for you.

Elijah lived at a time in history when miraculous experiences, prophecies, and visitations from God were "normal," everyday events. Elijah will show you how to access your inner wisdom so you can go beyond everyday limitations and embrace the expansive realm where magic and miracles live.

Traditionally during Passover, a special cup of wine is filled and put on the Seder table for Elijah. During the Seder, the door of the house is opened and everyone stands to allow Elijah the Prophet to enter and drink. A chair is also set aside for Elijah at every bris. At the conclusion of Shabbat, Jews sing about Elijah, hoping he will come "speedily, in our days…along with the Messiah, son of David, to redeem us." Elijah is a heroic figure in Jewish tradition.

In the New Testament, there are references that suggest Elijah had reincarnated as John the Baptist. In Islam, he is considered one of the prophets. In all three religions, he was seen as a very powerful man with a profound faith who was able to perform miracles. When a matter of law was at issue, Elijah was called upon to be the arbitrator.

Imagine what would happen in your life if you began to see miracles as normal, everyday events. Ask Elijah to allow you to see the world through his eyes if only for a moment.

White Buffalo Woman (mythological)

White Buffalo Woman will help you

- Make even the most mundane activities sacred
- Activate your sacred purpose
- Heal anything
- Create happiness, joy, and ease
- See the divine nature in everything

Invocation

When you want White Buffalo Woman to work with you, begin by calling on the four directions of north, east, south, and west. Ask for their blessing and guidance. Face the rising sun and call upon her. She will enfold you in her arms. When each of us is born, the universe sings our sacred song. She will sing it for you, reminding you of your divinity.

White Buffalo Woman is a holy woman who taught people how to walk through life in a sacred manner. She brought the sacred buffalo calf pipe to the Lakota and Sioux people. She will teach you how to live all of life in harmony with everything, which will fill you with a sense of peace and joy. When you move through life in a sacred manner, abundance, happiness, and joy are sure to follow.

White Buffalo Woman has promised to help human beings until they no longer need her assistance. She sees the light of the Great Spirit in everything and in everyone. She put the divine spark of love in the first human being and continues to help it to grow within each person. She will help you fan that spark of light into a brilliant flame that will illuminate your way, guiding you and directing you unerringly toward your freedom, happiness, and joy.

She has the ability to touch the essence of who you are and activate your inner wisdom and illuminate your sacred life's purpose. Once you align with that purpose, the entire world opens up to you. Ease becomes the cornerstone of your life and success unfolds before you. Ask for her assistance and be prepared to live in a sacred manner.

Maha Cohan (multiple incarnations)

Maha Cohan will help you

- Open your heart
- Deepen your connection to yourself and your spirit
- Find a career that makes your heart sing
- Resolve childhood issues

Invocation

When you call upon Maha Cohan, imagine yourself being enfolded by the wings of a great white dove. His help will gently flutter into your life. He often works with crystals. You can use your favorite stone or buy a crystal specifically for working with him. Hold it in your hand and call his name. Simply state your request and then be open to his guidance.

Maha Cohan is called the messenger, and he is the representative of the Holy Spirit. It is that spirit that gives life to everything, even the rocks, plants, and animals. Maha Cohan works closely with the angelic realms, bringing comfort and strength. When you open your heart to him, you can feel the pulsing presence of spirit and begin to align with the heart of God.

Maha Cohan's name means "great lord," and he has the incredible ability to create clear and open communication between your mind and your spirit. Once that dialogue has begun, change becomes so much easier that magic and miracles become part of everyday life. He will bring comfort and purity into your life. He brings balance and harmony into the dualities of feminine and masculine, love and fear, heaven and earth.

Maha Cohan greets each person as they are born and when they die. He is a gatekeeper and has always been with you. Since you have free will, he won't interfere in your life unless you ask. As soon as you call upon him, he will immediately share all his wisdom and light with you. He is a gentle and loving teacher, but he is very firm with his students. He expects you to follow through on his suggestions because he knows they will deepen your connection with your divine purpose and help to set you free.

Babaji

Babaji will help you

- Realize the power of love
- Overcome any challenge
- Overcome ignorance

Invocation

Babaji will often appear in your meditations as a violet flame or a beautiful lotus flower emanating brilliant light. Call upon him and ask for his guidance, love, and wisdom. Light a purple candle and invite him to be your teacher. When you call upon him, you may feel an immense wave of love suddenly flowing through you. Babaji beams an intense light of love at all who open their hearts to his presence.

Babaji is a name that has been applied to masters and sages throughout time. Baba means "father," and "ji" is a suffix of respect. Paramahansa Yogananda wrote about Babaji in his book, *Autobiography of a Yogi*. Babaji chose to forgo ascension until everyone on Earth has achieved freedom. He is also called "the Great One." He is said to have lived for thousands of years in various caves in the Himalayas. He watches over mankind and appears to people when they need his help.

Many people report having seen Babaji during the last two centuries. Nearly everyone describes him as a tall and slender young man. He has a noble appearance but is humble and loving with a childlike delight in life. When several people see him simultaneously, they each describe a different person. He speaks very little, seldom eats, and never sleeps. Babaji can display superhuman strength. He always talks to a person in his or her native language and can appear and disappear suddenly.

People are attracted to Babaji because of the bliss they experience in his presence. He is a master of love. He commands the profound wisdom of accomplished yogis, to whom everything is possible. Yogis are able to transcend the body, walk on fire, meditate endlessly, and live only on *prana* (energy).

When you call upon Babaji, he will be there. He invites you to demand proof of his presence. He will show you the path of truth and help you avoid getting lost in the illusion of false prophets.

John the Baptist (10 B.C.E.–28 C.E.)

John the Baptist will help you

- Detoxify your body
- Release old beliefs
- Purify your thoughts
- Deepen your faith

Invocation

Call on John the Baptist when you want a new beginning. He will bring order to your life, guide you, and direct you. Sprinkle some water around and ask for his assistance. Clean your home as a symbol of your commitment. Take a long, cleansing shower while asking John to fill you with the power of your divine self. You can also ask for his assistance every time you bathe or take a shower.

John was a man of profound faith, and his message was one of faith, purity, piety, and spiritual freedom. He was a bridge between the Old and New Testaments in the Bible. Factual knowledge about the life of John the Baptist is limited. He was a prophet calling for change. There were many groups practicing baptism at that time in history. Baptism is a form of ritualistic purification. It is symbolic of the purity of mind necessary to fully connect with one's spirit. John viewed baptism as a rededication to one's spiritual path. He took the wisdom of the past and the promise of the future and combined them into a beautiful ceremony that empowers the individual to step more fully into his or her own unique divine wisdom.

John asks you: What parts of your life are working, and what areas need to be transformed? Who are you, and what is it that you really want to create? John said, "I am a voice crying out in the wilderness." He cries out to you and invites you to celebrate your perfection and release any judgments you have about yourself. He invites you to go beyond your human frailty.

John was beheaded. Symbolically, he asks you to let go of your mind's limiting beliefs and embrace the wisdom that lies within your heart.

Merlin (mythological)

Merlin will help you

- Reconnect with your ability to perform miracles
- Create heaven on earth
- Find a lost love
- Attract abundance
- Know your godlike nature

Invocation

Even though Merlin is a wizard, there is no need to find a wand or gaze into a crystal ball. Simply call his name and then listen for his guidance. He may speak to you in symbols or leave a trail of signs to follow. Know you were born of magic; know Merlin will be there for you and he will.

Merlin was King Arthur's benefactor and a powerful wizard. Magicians play with molding, sculpting, and directing energy with a particular purpose in mind. Merlin was a magician, mystic, philosopher, Druid, shaman, monk, storyteller, bard, and astronomer. He was well known for his predictions, which always came true. Legend has it that Merlin's father was an angel who slept with a nun and gifted her with a child. He was an amazing teacher and guide for Arthur. He is more than willing to play the same role for anyone who is courageous enough to call upon him.

If you are thinking about asking Merlin for his assistance, he has probably been calling you for sometime. Merlin searches the world looking for souls willing to assist him in bringing magic back into the world. Merlin understands the illusionary nature of reality and seeks students with the wisdom and courage to go beyond the illusion and create a world based on the principles of Camelot. He knows what is possible and is willing to help anyone with similar goals.

Merlin knows that one of the most important ingredients to create what you want in life is a profound connection to your spirit. He knows that if you have a willingness to surrender the will of the small self for the benefit of the greater good and a heart willing to love, you already are a magician. When you call upon him, expect the unexpected. He will reawaken the wizard and master magician you have always been. He will remind you of your ability to consciously create whatever you want, whenever you want it. He will also teach you about the responsibilities inherent in being a creator.

Serapis Bay (multiple incarnations)

Serapis Bay will help you

- Bring harmony and balance into your life
- Make completing tasks easy
- Overcome procrastination
- Heighten your creativity
- Enhance your sex life

Invocation

Serapis Bay will help you bring the best of yourself forward. He will help you see the perfection in even your greatest flaws. Light a yellow candle and focus your attention on its light. Breathe in the golden glow and mentally release any fear or limiting thoughts. Then say a prayer and ask Serapis Bay for his assistance. Be sure to accomplish any tasks he assigns you. Remember that spiritual practice requires ongoing discipline and dedication if it is going to make a difference in your life.

Serapis Bay is an ascended master with the qualities of purity, discipline, joy, hope, and excellence. He is one of the great teachers of ascension on the planet. Closely associated with the Divine Mother, he helps to illuminate her gifts. He is often associated with Luxor in Egypt, and he holds open the Temple doors on the etheric level.

Serapis Bay encourages discipline and dedication in everyone who works with him. He will show you the shortest and most efficient path to enlightenment. He will help prepare you to manifest magic and miracles in your life and in the lives of those around you. He will initiate you into the ways of spirit and bless your life with a profound sense of harmony and beauty.

Serapis Bay works with the kundalini energy stored at the base of your spine. He will help you release this energy and guide you as this energy moves through your energy centers. Often the process of awakening kundalini energy can be unsettling. Serapis Bay will assist you in releasing this energy in a balanced and harmonious manner, which will gradually awaken the fire of your kundalini.

He also works with the yellow ray of creative intelligence, helping to bring out the creativity, focus, and freedom of artists, musicians, peacemakers, philosophers, and metaphysicians. He works to encourage balance and activate harmony and artistic beauty in all areas of life.

Jesus

(ca. 2 B.C.E.–28 C.E.)

Jesus will help you

- Connect with your own divinity, the Holy Spirit
- Heal your mind, body, and spirit
- Know you are God

- Release all beliefs in the idea that we are separate beings
- Perform miracles

Invocation

You can connect with Jesus through prayer and meditation. He is more than willing to help you enliven and enlighten your spirit so you too can see yourself as you truly are. When you open your heart to him, you will be filled with a wisdom and love that is all-encompassing. He will empower you to heal your life and change your world. He truly loves helping people realize the inherent power and wisdom that lies in everyone's heart and mind.

Although the idea of ascension predates Christianity, Jesus is perhaps the most famous story of ascension. Throughout history, there have been men and women who have transcended their limiting beliefs, reached a higher state of spiritual awareness, and dedicated themselves to being of service to humanity. Jesus is an incredible example of what human beings are capable of doing. An ascended master is a person who has experienced ascension, and all human beings have the potential to ascend. He often reminded his disciples that they were capable of doing miracles, just as he was. He is an amazing example of what can be done when a person dedicates his or her life to developing and maintaining a deep and abiding connection to spirit and the divine.

Jesus taught about love and forgiveness and the futility of judgment. He reminded people to turn the other cheek and taught them about the power of the Holy Spirit. He was a light willing and able to enlighten all people. He often talked about the Trinity, and one of the trinities he referred to was love, wisdom, and power. Jesus showed us that it is possible for everyone to obtain and express mastery. He was able to raise the dead, change water into wine, and calm the sea because he had aligned himself with his divinity. Jesus saw himself as he really was, a divine spark of God. He had stopped believing his mind's perspective that he was his body.

Buddha

(563–483 B.C.E.)

Buddha will help you

- Quiet your mind
- See the truth
- Release your limiting beliefs
- Experience compassion and love
- By being your spiritual guide if you are committed to the path of enlightenment

Invocation

Buddha is always at the edge of your reality waiting to be of assistance. Spend time in meditation, quieting your mind and asking for Buddha's guidance. Listen carefully for the gentle whispers. Tuning into your Buddha nature takes practice, so meditate often. As with all spiritual practices, the more you practice the better you will get at it.

Buddha is a Sanskrit word meaning "awakened." The most widely known Buddha is Siddhartha Gautama. Yet the term *Buddha* doesn't refer to any one individual, but rather to *any* human who has become enlightened. A Buddha is a person who sees life as it really is. He or she has awakened from the illusion most people live within. There have been numerous Buddhas, and there will be many more in the future. Buddhas reveal the path to bliss and show people how to connect with their own Buddha nature.

Due to the heightened awareness of consciousness, a Buddha sees the past, present, and future simultaneously and with neutrality, clarity, and great compassion. A Buddha embraces all beings with intense unconditional love. When given Buddha's blessing, animals become more peaceful. A Buddha is so deeply connected to his or her divine self that a Buddha responds from endless virtue. Just as the moon shines without effort, a Buddha acts naturally from loving compassion, without the confusion of undisciplined thought. A life based in loving-kindness and service flows from the Buddha nature.

For a Buddha, the trained mind is a wonderful tool instead of an incessant taskmaster. By quieting the mind, a Buddha sees life with loving compassion and is free of judgment. Enlightened beings delight in working with individuals as teachers and spirit guides. Buddhas are ordinary people who show each of us how to achieve the absolute bliss of Buddhahood. They can help awaken the path to the Buddha nature within us all. Through practice, you will also become an emissary of loving-kindness in the world.

Mary Magdalene (0–60 C.E.?)

Mary Magdalene will help you

- Feel the power of love
- Forgive
- See life with greater understanding and clarity
- Deepen your connection to your spirit
- Improve your psychic abilities

Invocation

Mary Magdalene has a huge heart and capacity to love. When you want her aid, write your request on a red piece of paper and light a white candle. Then say, "Mary, please help me in my quest to create happiness and joy. Allow me to be of service and to know what actions to take. Mary, help me to know true love and share it with everyone I touch."

Mary Magdalene was the most important female disciple of Jesus. Traditionally she has been labeled as a prostitute, although the Bible doesn't support that view. Some people believe she was the wife of Jesus and that they had a daughter named Sarah. Regardless of what you believe about her, she is a very powerful teacher. Her message is one of love, gratitude, and deliverance.

She reminds us of the importance of loving ourselves and of being of service to others. She was present at the crucifixion of Jesus and was the first to see him after he rose from the dead. The Gospel of Mary Magdalene reveals Mary's profound understanding of the teachings of Jesus. Her gospel survived until early in the third century but was dismissed and despised by the early church fathers. The Gospel of Mary Magdalene has what might be considered Taoist and Buddhist principles presented in first-century Christian language. Interestingly, the first gospel written by a woman was one of the first to be dismissed by the early church.

Mary fully understood the profound message of Jesus and asks us to embrace those teachings as a way of life. Forgiveness, generosity of spirit, the understanding of the perfection of all of life, and the importance of love are heavily emphasized by Mary. Her heart is always open and her wisdom is only a thought away.

Samuel

(ca. 1000 B.C.E.)

Samuel will help you

- Release your judgments
- See life in a more expansive manner
- Develop a green thumb
- Heal any emotional wounds

Invocation

Samuel will show you how to quiet your mind as you learn to listen for the voice of your spirit. Spend some time meditating. Just focus your attention on your breathing, and when you are distracted by your thoughts, return your attention to your breath. You will continue to have thoughts, but just keep bringing your attention back to your breath.

Ask Samuel to help you and he will come to you.
Open your heart, quiet your mind, and allow love to be your guide.

Samuel is called the "knowledgeable prophet" and is recognized by followers of Islam, Judaism, and Christianity. He began to hear voices at night and at first thought his father Eli was speaking to him. Eventually he realized it was the voice of God. In the classical sense, Samuel extolled people to repent and turn to God as their salvation. He traveled around the countryside preaching fear in the name of God. When he ascended, he realized fear was an illusion and that God's love was unconditional and free of judgment as well as expansive.

As an ascended master, Samuel reminds people that their freedom lies in activating their inner wisdom and listening to the voice of their spirit. He assists people in activating that connection through the power of love. He reminds us that judgment weakens our connection to our divinity and shows us how to see all of life through the eyes of perfection.

Samuel knows that meditation is one of the most powerful and affective ways to connect with your spirit. He will assist you in developing the necessary focus to meditate and finding the type of meditation that will be most effective for you. Just ask for his assistance.

Lanto

(multiple incarnations)

Lanto will help you

- Create abundance in all areas of your life
- Fine-tune your ability to manifest
- Speak eloquently
- Release beliefs that no longer serve you
- Deepen your understanding of your true nature

Invocation

When you want to invite Lanto into your life, begin by meditating on the golden lotus flame that is symbolic of his presence. Light a golden-colored candle and imagine yourself seated in the center of a beautiful lotus flower. Allow Lanto to light your path while he guides your thoughts and behaviors. Visualize the golden flame transforming any limiting thoughts or feelings and infusing them with love.

Lanto is the ascended master who teaches about true wisdom, understanding, and the drawbacks of judgment. Lord Lanto delights in showing people how to attain enlightenment and how to connect with the Holy Spirit's gifts of wisdom and knowledge. He will show you how to use discernment so you can make choices that are beneficial to all who are involved.

Many of Lanto's incarnations were in China, where he infused that country's culture with great wisdom and love. Lanto will remind you of your basic self-worth and innate wisdom. He reminds people to love themselves unconditionally and to remember that connecting with their divinity is a process. Lanto feels that one of the many gifts of earthly life is the opportunity to see the results of our thoughts and beliefs in three-dimensional physical reality. Lanto knows life is an opportunity to make choices, see the results of those choices, and then choose again. Moment by moment, there is an opportunity to practice the loving presence of spirit or to fall deeper into the illusion of separation.

Lord Lanto sees human beings as gods who are in the process of remembering their divinity. He reminds each individual to celebrate their greatness and lovingly release their limiting beliefs about themselves. He emphasizes love, joy, and laughter. When you invite his guidance into your life, his beaming smile will light up your life.

Abraham

(ca. 2000 B.C.E.)

Abraham will help you

- Understand the power of faith
- Find your life's purpose

- Remember your basic goodness and divine nature

Invocation

Abraham was a man of prayer. He spent a lot of time talking to God. Ask Abraham to show you how to have faith, how to let go of your fearful thinking and feel the love of the universe embracing you. Walk under the stars and imagine what it must have been like for Abraham to live in the desert. Then open your heart and expect miracles to happen.

Abraham plays a pivotal role in Judaism, Christianity, and Islam. These religions are sometimes referred to as the Abrahamic religions. In Judaism, Abraham is the revered patriarch. In Christianity, Abraham is a spiritual forbearer. In Islam, Abraham is regarded as another important prophet in a line that began with Adam.

God promised Abraham he would found a nation and have millions of descendants. Yet Abraham was one hundred years old when his wife, Sarah, bore him a son. Then God asked Abraham to sacrifice this beloved son. Another man, asked to sacrifice his son, would have become hostile and bitter. Many would have rebuked God and turned away. Instead, Abraham trusted God and was shown the power of love when God spared his son, replacing his sacrifice with a sheep.

Abraham reminds us of the power of sustaining our convictions. He exemplifies the power of faith and perspective. When you aren't sure what to do next, ask Abraham for his guidance. He is a leader and a founder of movements. He has the capacity to harness his profound faith and work wonders. So ask for his help, open your heart, and trust the guidance you receive. His guidance will always be loving, gentle, and kind.

Jeremiah

(ca. 580 B.C.E.)

Jeremiah will help you

- Let go of all limitations
- Be truly happy and free

- Heal your mind, body, and spirit

Invocation

Jeremiah realizes that the process of surrender for most human beings can be an arduous one. He knows that most humans are fiercely independent, and surrender seems to fly in the face of that independence. He suggests starting by asking for the ability to love and accept yourself completely just the way you are. Then gently move toward the act of surrendering to your divine will. Once you feel the power of that love, nothing and no one can ever prevent you from having peace of mind and joy at all times.

Call upon him, ask to feel loved, and then just open your heart and receive his love.
Jeremiah asks you to let him love you until you can love yourself.

Jeremiah lived in Jerusalem when the Babylonians had taken control of the city. He lived through the invasion, the deportations and slaughter of Jews, and the destruction of the Temple. He had the choice of staying in Judah or going to Babylon. He chose to stay in Judah but was forced to later flee to Egypt. The book of Jeremiah is mostly biographical and historical in nature. He spoke of the importance of personal spirituality versus organized religion and the necessity of individuals taking responsibility. These two teachings were revolutionary in his day and constituted a great step forward.

He shows people how freedom, happiness, and joy are easily obtained by embracing divine will and how they remain elusive when a person isn't willing to take responsibility for his or her actions. Jeremiah explains divine will as an alignment with a person's higher purpose and true spiritual nature. Divine will is something inherent and internal within each human being. It isn't a desire by some external power to force you to do their will. By surrendering to your true nature, you are infused with the all-powerful force of love. With love, anything is possible.

Sanat Kumara (ca. 1000 B.C.E.)

Sanat Kumara will help you

- Light the sacred fire within your own heart
- Cleanse your home and your life of negative influences
- Awaken your divinity
- Enliven your relationships
- Create abundance
- Balance your male and female aspects

Invocation

Light a beautiful pine-scented candle as you call upon Sanat Kumara.
Call on him once a day for a week, and he will teach you discernment
and show you how to connect with the Divine Mother.

Sanat Kumara is responsible for the evolutionary path of the Earth and all souls incarnated on this planet, including humans, plants, and animals. He works very closely with the angelic realm. Sanat Kumara is the guardian of the sacred flame. The tradition of the Yule log originated with Sanat Kumara's custom of consecrating the sacred fires every year. Each year he would rekindle the sacred fires, and people would come from all around the world to rekindle their fires from the sacred source.

Sanat Kumara actualizes the numerous facets of the divine self in physical reality. He invites you to embrace all of the aspects of yourself and surrender to the compassionate nature of your true self.

Sanat Kumara is called the "holder of all wisdom and learning." He helps to destroy all negative tendencies that weaken one's connection to the divine self. He bestows spiritual gifts on all who call upon him, especially the power of discernment. He will also help awaken the Divine Mother within you. He is often seen as a four-petal white lotus flower that resides at the base of a person's spine. He is the essence of the sacred fire that gives life to you.

Sanat Kumara banishes ignorance and replaces it with divine wisdom and love. He is a bright light and a loving guide who will assist you whenever you are ready to let go of your limitations. He is a miracle worker and loves to remind people how to create miracles in their own lives.

Lady Nada (multiple incarnations)

Lady Nada will help you

- Develop true self-mastery
- Protect children
- Empower and guide teachers, ministers, and healers
- Bring justice into life's more challenging events

Invocation

Just by calling her name you will feel her loving presence. Lady Nada is an incredible loving and powerful being to have in your life. If you would like her to work with you on a regular basis, light a deep red, rose-scented candle each day and invite her into your life. She will help you in surprising and miraculous ways.

Lady Nada's message is one of peace and brotherhood, devotion, humility, selflessness, service, and wisdom born of love. She reminds all humans that they are a ray of pure, unconditional love. She believes it is very important to remember that you are not your personality, you are not your habitual behaviors, and you are not the sum total of your experiences. You are a spiritual entity, a divine spark of love.

Lady Nada helps individuals see the truth. She will help you reconnect with the essence of who and what you really are. Separateness is not a reality, and it is the illusion created by our beliefs. Beloved Lady Nada will show you the truth and help you embrace your personality self rather than make it an adversary. No matter what the issue, love is always the answer. Nada reminds us that whatever we resist becomes stronger, and whatever we embrace and love dissolves into the nothingness from which it came.

In her last incarnation, she was the priestess in the Temple of Love. Nada often works with the rose as a symbol of enlightenment. Just as a rose starts as a tiny bud, slowly unfurling into a magnificent flower, so each spirit unfolds in its own way into a magnificent being of light. Nada asks you the following questions: Where do you want to focus your energy? Do you want to use your energy to focus on your feelings of separation and deepen your connection to the personality self? Or would you rather use your energy to strengthen your ability to love and, in the process, deepen your connection to your spirit?

El Morya

(multiple incarnations)

El Morya will help you

- Manifest your life's purpose
- Speak your truth in a loving manner
- Receive all the gifts the universe has to offer

Invocation

El Morya is master of the blue ray, so when you want to call upon him, light a blue candle. Sprinkle some sandalwood oil in your hands and rub them together. Then place your palms together and hold your hands in front of your heart. Rest your nose on the tips of your fingers and close your eyes. Take a few slow, deep breaths to get centered. Then ask El Morya to help you align your mind and your heart with your Higher Self. Spend some time surrendering and letting go.

El Morya is an ascended master who was born a Rajput prince in India. Very little is known of his life. He became a monk and spent much of his time in monasteries in the Himalayas. He founded the Theosophical Society. His most profound teachings are a powerful synthesis of the ancient spiritual truths of the East with the traditions of the West.

El Morya had many incarnations on Earth. His devotion to God is a theme that runs through all of them. His profound love allows his wisdom to reach across the veil between worlds. He continues to teach anyone who has an open heart and is willing to connect. El Morya's most important message is about the use of our will. He shows people how powerful it is to align your will with God's will. This divine will is a powerful stream of love. As we surrender and align with that will, we eventually reunite with our Higher Self.

He reminds people that God's greatest gift to human beings is free will. God doesn't have a plan for individuals; God's only desire for us is that we reunite with the essence of who and what we really are. When a person is aligned with the will of God, success is sure to follow. People experience hardships and suffering only when they have lost their connection to the divine.

Mother Mary

Mother Mary will help you

- Love unconditionally
- Feel connected
- Heal your relationships
- Create abundance
- Follow your bliss

Invocation

Roses are sacred to Mary, and for centuries, people have used rosary beads when praying to her. Prayer beads are common in many traditions and can be a useful tool for focusing your attention. If you feel called to use them, do so. If not, simply ask Mary for her help and she will be there. She is the beloved Mother who is always nearby, at the edge of your reality waiting for you to invite her closer.

Mother Mary has many names and has appeared in many forms to all of mankind. She is the ultimate symbol of divine love. Her capacity to love is beyond most humans' ability to fathom. Her perfect love can cast out all of your fears and allow you to reach your highest potential. Her perfect, unconditional love will allow you to let go of your limiting beliefs, including any beliefs you have about yourself and the world that cause you to reject the abundance life freely offers you. Mary will remind you that you are a limitless being of light and that all of your limitations and all of your suffering are caused by your belief in separation.

Mary will show you how to bring to fruition a life based on a divine connection and a profound knowing of your oneness with everyone and to everything in the universe. She will teach you how to create heaven on earth by letting go of your old self-image and embracing God's image of you instead. Her love is so unconditional and all-encompassing that she sees only the perfection in everyone and everything.

Open your heart and your mind to her. Ask for the willingness to completely surrender any beliefs you have about yourself, and see life from her perspective. Notice your judgments and ask Mary to help you see things differently. When you feel fear, ask her to fill you with love. If you ask Mary for her help but instead focus on your old beliefs, she can't help you. So ask for her help with an open heart and an open mind.

Rainbow People (mythological)

Rainbow People will help you

- Heal childhood traumas
- Release the pain and anger of betrayal
- Connect with your inner wisdom
- Lighten up and feel joy

Invocation

Rainbow People are so willing to help that all you have to do is call upon them.
They are powerful guides and healers, so you might want to have them in your life
on a regular basis. As a reminder, put some rainbow stickers up on your mirrors.
When they work with you, expect to see rainbows in some of the most unusual places.

Rainbow People are angelic beings of light that exist solely to help people. They live on the ethereal, or spiritual, plane beyond the awareness of human beings. The Rainbow People are very compassionate. They love human beings with all their hearts. They have the knowledge of the ages and are willing to share that wisdom with anyone who asks. They teach a great deal about forgiveness and understanding.

When they lower their vibration to work with mortals, they appear as a brilliant white-gold light. They have the ability to assist people in opening their hearts and their minds. If you call upon them, you will immediately feel uplifted. They will fill you with a profound sense of acceptance and gratitude. Rainbow People are miracle workers when it comes to old childhood traumas. They will help you to forgive and release the past so you can see the freedom that it's possible to gain from the experience.

They are able to bring their ancient wisdom into your life in a way that can profoundly transform your way of being in the world. They will help you see everything from a more limitless perspective so you can make better choices.

Mahatma Gandhi (1869–1948)

Mahatma Gandhi will help you

- End an abusive relationship
- Improve your leadership abilities
- Find a great job
- Create inner peace and harmony

Invocation

Mahatma Gandhi is a humble and simple man. He changed a nation with the power of his conviction and love. To ask for his assistance, light a small white candle and explain your dilemma. Sit quietly for a few minutes and wait for his inspiration to motivate you.

Mahatma Gandhi was born Mohandas Karamchand Gandhi in Porbandar, India. The Indian people called him Mahatma, which means "Great Soul." Using nonviolent resistence, he led the Indian people out of British colonial rule and became one of the most respected spiritual and political leaders of the 1900s. Gandhi developed a method of direct social action based upon the principles of courage, nonviolence, and truth called Satyagraha. He thought that the way people behaved was much more important than what they achieved. Satyagraha promoted nonviolence and civil disobedience as the most appropriate methods for obtaining political and social goals.

Mahatma Gandhi lived what he taught. A woman traveled a great distance to have Gandhi convince her daughter to stop eating sugar. He listened very patiently to the woman and her daughter and then told her to come back the following week. She once again traveled all day to reach him. He invited them to sit. He looked at the daughter and said, "Stop eating sugar." The woman became very annoyed with him and asked why he couldn't have done that the preceding week. He said, "Madam, last week I was still eating sugar." Gandhi also spun cloth every day and believed in simplicity and the local manufacture of goods.

He will show you how to change your life without unnecessary struggle. In a gentle yet powerful manner, he will guide you to personal freedom and a life filled with love, happiness, and joy. He will help you see that all true power arises from love and a connection to spirit.

Isaiah

(eight century B.C.E.)

Isaiah will help you

- Connect with your own inner wisdom
- Open your heart to true love
- Find real happiness
- Engage the power of faith
- Release fear

Invocation

Isaiah loves music and joyful singing. Roll up the windows in your car and sing your request at the top of your lungs. It doesn't matter if you can't carry a tune; just sing loudly with complete abandon, pour out all of your hopes and dreams, and let Isaiah help you manifest them.

Isaiah is one of the most renowned prophetic visionaries. He lived in Jerusalem during one of the most turbulent periods in history. He was one of the most political prophets, and due to his social status, he played an active role in the course of events. Regardless of the tumultuous events happening around him, he consistently put his faith in the power of the divine. Even though almost all of the neighboring states were constantly attacking one another, he remained at peace.

Many of his prophecies foretold the coming of the messiah. He extolled people to follow the path of truth and love and to forsake the path of anger and violence. He believed people's spiritual tenacity would set them free.

He encouraged others to invite the love of God into their lives and thus be assured of happiness and success. He believed God's love was available to all who opened their hearts and allowed themselves to be embraced by that all-encompassing love.

The messiah referred to by Isaiah is the enlightened being who lives within each person. Isaiah reminds us that we are our own saviors. You save yourself by finding the answers that lie within your own heart. Asking or expecting someone else to save you is the antithesis of enlightenment. Opening your heart, connecting to your spirit, and allowing God into your life is the path that set Isaiah free and will set you free.

Saint Germain   (multiple incarnations)

Saint Germain will help you

- Expand your ability to experience unconditional love
- Use the gift of prophecy
- Make freedom a reality in your life
- Deepen your connection to your divinity

Invocation

Imagine yourself being filled with a brilliant violet light. Feel each and every cell of your body vibrating with the essence of the energy of transformation. Stand in the violet light until you feel Saint Germain's loving presence. Then ask him for his assistance. Ask him to show you how to see life from the perspective of your Higher Self rather than the loveless perspective of your small self. Say a simple prayer and open up to Saint Germain's assistance. He will be there for you.

The Ascended Master Saint Germain teaches that the highest form of alchemy is to transform one's limited, fearful human consciousness into the limitless and unconditional loving divinity of the Higher Self. He stands ready to assist everyone in this endeavor. He reminds all who are willing to listen that the only difference between an ascended master and a mortal is that the master has chosen to be free while humans have not yet made that decision. Freedom is a choice we make moment by moment by how we choose to focus our attention, what we choose to believe, and whether we chose love or fear as our motivation.

Saint Germain is the master teacher of freedom, alchemy, justice, mercy, and transmutation. He brings the gifts of prophecy and the ability to perform miracles to souls willing to transform their thinking. He uses love as the catalyst for all change. He brings the violet flame of transformation into the world to help people lay the foundation for a life of freedom and joy. He reminds us that a person's birthright is happiness and that we live in a limitless universe that is safe and abundant.

Saint Germain is also here on Earth to invite all nations to put behind them the destructive uses of science and religion. He invites them to learn how to use science and religion to help all human beings to experience enlightenment.

King Arthur (mythological)

King Arthur will help you

- Connect with your magic potential
- Find love
- Infuse your life with integrity
- Manifest your dreams

Invocation

Light a candle and ask Arthur to reveal his presence to you. Ask for his help and know he will be there for you. You may feel a gentle warmth or notice a breeze rustling your hair. Write out your desires and then burn them. Allow the fire to transform your wishes into reality.

King Arthur's name conjures up images of magic, wizards, and noble deeds of bravery and love. The mystical elements of the story of Arthur are filled with moral wisdom and reminders of the endless possibilities life contains. The struggle between good and evil and the promise of the return of magic speaks to a place deep within each person's spirit. The relationship between Arthur and Merlin has profound lessons to share. The quest for the Holy Grail symbolically represents the search to deepen the connection to the divinity and our own spiritual quest.

King Arthur is a powerful teacher and guide. His dedication to the creation of Camelot, his relationship with Merlin, and his ability to love have much to teach us. King Arthur's legend is steeped in mystery and magic along with the power of love and a heart dedicated to honesty and truth. The Lady of the Lake teaches about power, honor, and dedication. The Sword in the Stone reminds us of the power of integrity and truth. In one brief and shining moment, you too can change your life and transform your world.

Arthur guides you with his deep commitment to justice, honor, and love. When you first heard about the legend of King Arthur, what was your first reaction? Did you yearn to spend time with Merlin? To sit at the round table or hold Excalibur in your hands? How did the story affect you? Now ask yourself what hurdles you want to overcome in your life.

Job (mythological)

Job will help you

- Connect with your spirit
- Develop discernment
- Manifest your heart's desires
- Heal a broken relationship
- Improve your health

Invocation

Job's main focus is the importance of having a profound connection to the divine. First ask Job to help you find a way to connect with your spirit on a daily basis. Once you have decided on a daily practice, take time each day to do it. Continue to call upon Job and he will help you deepen the connection until it becomes the background noise in your life. Once you have that connection and maintain it, anything is possible.

Job is probably the oldest book in the Bible. The name Job is itself an ancient name. Job poses and then answers the question, "Why do bad things happen to good people?" The story of Job seems to be one of suffering and faith. God allowed Satan to take away all his riches, livestock, home, servants, and children, yet he retained his faith. Job's message is that regardless of life's circumstances, we can be happy as long as we maintain our connection to our spirit. He reminds people that they are responsible for their choices in life. We are sovereign beings with free will. The universe doesn't test us; God doesn't cause ill health or give us abundance or remove it from our life. Life happens, and then you make a series of choices.

Job reminds us that we are the creators in our world. No matter what you ask the universe for, it has only one answer, "Yes." The problem is that what we think we are asking for is often far different from what we are actually asking for. What we ask for is based on and colored by our beliefs, assumptions, and agreements.

Job reminds us to use our connection to our spirit as a touchstone, as our compass, our guide, and our comfort. Your spirit speaks to you through your heart's desires. Job teaches you how to know the difference between the voice of your spirit and the voice of your fear-based small self. Job teaches about the power of faith and the importance of being grateful for everything in life, even what we might perceive as suffering. He reminds us that health, happiness, and abundance come directly from a deep and profound connection to our spirit.

Paramahansa Yogananda (1893–1952)

Paramahansa Yogananda will help you

- Bring a spiritual perspective to all of life
- Find your life's work
- Develop your creativity
- Improve your memory
- Release stress and fear

Invocation

Paramahansa Yogananda emphasized the importance of meditation, so take a few minutes to focus your attention on your breathing. Quiet your mind and allow yourself to go within. Then ask him to help you feel the connection, talk to him about your concerns, and ask for his help. You will be amazed at the power of love to heal your life.

Paramahansa Yogananda wrote the book *Autobiography of a Yogi* and created the Self-Realization Fellowship. To his most serious students, he introduced Kriya Yoga to assist them in awakening their spirit. Mahatma Gandhi requested to be initiated by Yogananda when they met. He was a gentle man full of love and compassion. Just by being in his presence, people reported feeling better. When you invite him into your life, you will immediately feel an opening in your heart and your fears and concerns will dissolve. He will help you open your heart so you can experience your true nature and the interdependence and interconnectedness of everyone and everything.

Paramahansa Yogananda's invitation to you is to embark upon an expansive, exciting, and miraculous pilgrimage to connect with your Divine Spirit. He is a beloved teacher who emphasized the underlying similarities of all of the world's religions. He saw them all as wonderful paths to enlightenment. He knew that it didn't matter what path people took to find their spiritual connection as long as they found that connection. His life and teachings are a continuing source of inspiration and light to all people of all races. His emphasis was showing people how to achieve a direct and personal experience of God.

When he died, his body was transported to all of his ashrams (teaching centers) without any means of preservation. When he was finally cremated almost a month later, there were absolutely no signs of deterioration in his body.

Lao-tze

(fourth century B.C.E.)

Lao-tze will help you

- Create balance in your life
- Invite abundance and ease
- Use harmony to manifest your wildest dreams
- Find love
- Enhance your relationships

Invocation

Lao-tze is a simple, humble, and wise man with a generous spirit and loving heart. Light a plain white candle and ask him for his assistance. His advice is always very simple and to the point. Once you have asked for his aid, watch out for the signs. He may even give you his answer in a fortune cookie or through a casual remark made by a friend.

Lao-tze is the author of the *Tao Te Ching* and founder of the Taoist religion in China. His name means "Old Master" and "Tao" means the "Way." Legend says that, saddened by the state of affairs, Lao-tze decided to leave China. As he was about to walk through the last gate in the great wall that protected the kingdom, the guard recognized him as the great philosopher. He wouldn't let him pass until he wrote down his wisdom and shared his philosophy. Lao-tze sat down and wrote down the eighty-one sayings that became the *Tao Te Ching*.

Lao-tze teaches a simple way of life that is in complete harmony with everything. His philosophy is all about acceptance, surrender, and a deep sense of connection. The "Tao" (pronounced "*Dow*") is an indefinable energy.

It is something that has to be experienced. It refers to a power that envelopes, surrounds, and flows through all things, living and nonliving. The Tao regulates natural processes and nurtures the balance that inherently exists in the entire universe. The Tao embodies the harmony of opposites. Lao-tze saw that the goal of life was to become one with the Tao.

He will help you embrace all of you and bring balance and harmony to your life. His gentleness and love are all-encompassing. Lao-tze's simplicity and his concise use of words will guide you and direct you. He will cut through life's complexity and show you the way to create a life of happiness and ease.

White Fire Eagle (mythological)

White Fire Eagle will help you

- See perfection
- Rise above limitation
- Develop perspective
- Connect with your divinity
- Heal

Invocation

Eagles are considered the messengers between the spirit world and humans. Look to the sky for messages when you ask White Fire Eagle for guidance and healing. Allow yourself to really watch a bird in flight. Imagine you are flying with him. Tell him where you want to go and feel the exhilaration of your powerful wings as he leads you there.

White Fire Eagle's message is that by flying above the earth, it's possible to see the big picture, the unity of all of life. The true nature of all beings shines a great light upon the world, which is easy to see when flying above it. This light brightens as we honor our holy natures.

White Fire Eagle knows creation is perfect. He sees that no beings are outside of the web of life. White Fire Eagle knows that humans, like spiders, weave the stories of their lives. He can show you how to weave the story you want to live.

White Fire Eagle will teach you the healing power of eagle feathers. He will show you how to circle above yourself and witness your own beauty and courage. His joy in flying is infectious. White Fire Eagle's healing begins as you stretch your wings and allow yourself to be lifted by the Great Spirit. He will show you how to catch the currents and fly. His great beating wings bring comfort and strength.

Kuthumi

(multiple incarnations)

Kuthumi will help you

- Attain self-mastery
- Release any limiting beliefs
- Clear out your subconscious mind
- Settle all karmic debts
- Fill your heart with divine love

Invocation

Kuthumi's mantra is, "I am light." He is of the light and infuses anyone who calls upon him with the glorious light of pure, unconditional love. Call his name and repeat his mantra. Silently repeating his mantra all day long will assist you in focusing on love and clearing your mind of limiting beliefs. Kuthumi will respond to his mantra and your request with his wisdom, power, and understanding.

Kuthumi was born in the early nineteenth century in Kashmir and attended Oxford University. He later met with Dr. Theodor Fechner, the father of modern psychology. Kuthumi helped found the Theosophical Society with El Morya. He spent his later years secluded in a lamasery in Tibet.

Kuthumi is the ascended master of love, wisdom, and understanding. He will help anyone who desires knowledge, especially during these times of change. Kuthumi is known as a master of psychology. He has dedicated himself to assisting humans overcome their limiting beliefs by bringing them into balance emotionally and spiritually. He helps raise people's awareness so personal growth is no longer a process of two steps forward and one backward. Through the power of his love, he is able to heal both the conscious and subconscious levels of the mind. Kuthumi is able to see the energy pattern caused by unresolved issues and to help a person channel that energy in a more productive manner.

He also plays sacred music of both the East and the West. These heavenly compositions are keyed to the music of the celestial spheres and assist people as they transition from life to death. This music allows souls to release all karmic bonds and anything that would hold them back from attaining their spiritual freedom.

Maitreya

Maitreya will help you

- Connect with your life's purpose
- Use love and cooperation to create anything
- Discover the perfect place to live
- Improve all of your relationships
- Find wonderful transportation

Invocation

To invite Maitreya into your life, float some rose petals in a beautiful bowl. Take a few deep breaths and call his name. Then explain your desires. He is always available, so after you ask him for help, open your heart and your mind and know he is there for you.

Lord Maitreya (pronounced "*my-tray-ah*") is sometimes called the "Master of Masters." Maitreya is the Buddha who has yet to leave the Earth; he is so dedicated to all beings that he has refused to enter nirvana (transcendence) until all beings achieve enlightenment. He is called "The Compassionate One." His essences have been expected for eons by all religions. Christians know him as the Christ and expect his return. Jews expect the Messiah; Hindus look for Krishna; Buddhists expect him as Maitreya Buddha; and Muslims anticipate the Messiah. He has shared his love in many forms throughout the eons.

Maitreya is often pictured as a laughing Buddha carrying a large hemp bag and surrounded by children. He is not a religious leader but prefers to be known as the Teacher. Maitreya hopes to inspire humanity to see itself as a family and come together to create a world based on sharing, social justice, and global cooperation. He wants to facilitate a world based on love, a sane world whose priorities are feeding all people and providing health care and education for everyone.

He will bring you inner peace and show you how to make choices that will open up unlimited opportunities. Maitreya teaches love and cooperation. His vision is expansive and compassionate. He sees the best in everyone and is able to see everything through eyes of love. He is a wonderful teacher and guide and can show you how to live a life beyond your wildest dreams. He will show you the real power of your spirit and the true path to holiness and peace.

Part IV

Gods, Goddesses, and Deities

Every culture has its own worldview and way of connecting with the divine. There is a great deal of similarity between most creation myths, and there are a variety of ways to explain that divinity. There are so many gods, goddesses, and deities. As you get to know them, you also learn about the people and the culture where they originated.

The gods and goddesses are always willing to help. In return, they expect you to open your heart and your mind to their love and to deepen your connection to your spirit. They know your perfection and know you are a spiritual being. They will never demand that you do anything, but they will suggest you take certain actions and spend some time developing your spiritual practices.

These beings that are called gods, goddesses, and deities have a very different perspective of life. Each one has been honored in a way that is consistent with their culture. The world is a much smaller place than it used to be. Wars were fought in defense of gods, and people were tortured and killed because of their beliefs. In the name of love there was a lot of bloodshed and violence.

Today there is so much more acceptance. You have the opportunity to work with any of the deities. Take some time to get to know them. If a particular god, goddess, or deity really resonates with you, perhaps explore that tradition in greater detail. Open your heart and allow yourself the gift of developing a deep and intimate connection with them and in the process with your own divinity.

Morrigan

Associated Culture

Celtic

Morrigan will help you

- Find balance
- Win in a legal matter
- Make sure your voice is heard
- Have a child

Invocation

Morrigan has a fierce sense of right and wrong and tries to bring balance to all situations. When you want to ask for her help, you can say, "Morrigan, please help me find peace and resolution. Help me [explain your request]. I give thanks for your creative solution and for the courage and wisdom to carry it out."

Morrigan is a goddess of battle, war, and fertility. She is closely related to Danu and is often part of a trio of goddesses. Her name means either the "Great Queen" or the "Phantom Queen." She was the dominant goddess in Europe before the Copper Age and was often referred to as the Great Goddess. She represents the crone aspect of the goddess. Morrigan loved sending men to war. At times she would hover over the battle in the shape of a crow. Wherever there was a war, you could find Morrigan. Her battle cry was said to be louder than a thousand men.

She is both the goddess of birth and of death, helping souls move through the cycles of life. Morrigan is also a healer and a proctor of the land. As with all Celtic goddesses, she is neither good nor evil but instead has elements of both and strives to balance them. By bringing death, she creates new life.

She is closely associated with the symbol of the horse. Morrigan is an intrinsic part of the land and protects it with her fierce loyalty and love. She is most useful when you want to get rid of someone who irritates you. She will also help you bring harmony to your family of origin.

Itzamna

Associated Culture

Mayan

Itzamna will help you

- Create ceremonies to facilitate healing
- Bring abundance into your life
- Connect with nature
- Harness your own divinity
- Let go of old emotional wounds

Invocation

Itzamna can assist you in many ways. He is a master at creating ritual, so you can invite him to help you create a ritual to help you become centered and to harness the energy of creation. Follow your intuition. If you feel like going outside, go outside. If you feel like lighting a candle, light one. Allow your inner wisdom to guide you as you create a powerful ritual for yourself.

Itzamna is the founder of the Mayan culture, the ruler of heaven, and one of the older Mayan gods. He brought his people maize and cocoa and showed them how to heal. He taught them the use of calendars and helped them solidify their culture. Itzamna is god of the sun and the moon, so he rules over both the day and the night. He is also known as the lord of knowledge. Itzamna is associated with the cardinal points of the compass and their accompanying colors (east, red; north, white; west, black; and south, yellow).

Itzamna often appears as a cultural hero. He showed human beings how to divide the land. He established rit-uals for religious worship. He is like a wonderful elder brother who gladly shows you the shortcuts and helps you avoid the pitfalls you might otherwise encounter.

Itzamna is one of the most important deities of Mayan mythology. As the god of maize and of day and night, he is truly the god of life and of creation. He can show you how to deeply transform your life and the life of your loved ones. You can't make another person change in order to make your life easier, but you can fill his or her heart with so much love that together you can create joy, happiness, and abundance.

Tara

Associated Cultures

Hindu / Buddhist / Tibetan

Tara will help you

- Create love in your life
- Stay protected from all harm
- Bring fertility into your life in all areas
- Overcome any obstacle
- Have compassion for yourself and others

Invocation

Tara is a powerful goddess with many faces. Her main desire is to help
you realize your own divine nature. Just call upon her, open your heart,
and humbly ask for her help. Tara is always just a thought away.
You may feel a growing warmth in your hands and feet as she embraces you.

The goddess Tara is honored in many different traditions. She is the symbol of eternal love and light in the Hindu tradition. She is the Buddhist "goddess of compassion," who teaches the wisdom of non-attachment. Tara is so highly regarded she is said to be the Mother of all the Buddhas. In Tibet, she is the goddess of love, born from her mother's tears of compassion for humanity's suffering. Tara's essential desire is to answer humans' pleas for assistance. Tara is a Sanskrit word meaning "Star."

The Tibetans know Tara as "The Faithful One." She is the loyal and fierce protector of her people. To this day, stories of her intervention and assistance are told by Tibetan refugees who fled the horrors of Chinese occupation.

In the mind-training practices offered by the great masters of Tibet, Tara is an archetype of our own inner wisdom. She speaks of a transformation of consciousness, a journey to freedom. The Tibetan masters teach many simple and direct means for each person to discover within themselves the wisdom, compassion, and glory that is Tara.

Tara is worshipped in many forms, but the best known are the peaceful and compassionate ones. White Tara, who protects and brings health, long life, and peace, is often worshipped. As is the dynamic Green Tara, who brings fertility to the earth, overcomes obstacles, and saves us from physical and spiritual danger.

Cronos

Cronos will help you

- Manifest anything
- Have prophetic dreams

- Remember to be loving and generous
- Get through emotionally difficult times

Invocation

Cronos often works in the dream state, so ask for his help just before you go to sleep. Get a clear picture of what you would like him to create and then ask him to use his skills to create it. He was able to create heaven and earth, so he can certainly help you manifest your dreams.

Cronos was the child of Gaia (Mother Earth) and Ouranos (the sky god). After he killed his father, Cronos became the King of the Titans. The Titans were a race of gods that created the universe and all the Olympian gods. Cronos later served as the model that gave birth to the mythical figure of Father Time.

All in all, Cronos was a happy but rather insecure god. He had a dream one night that his children would overthrow him. He told his wife Rhea about the dream, and she told him to forget it. He didn't listen to her and decided to get rid of his children by eating them. He was able to eat all of them except Zeus. His wife hid Zeus and fed Cronos a rock instead. Many years later, when Zeus had grown up, he gave Cronos a potion that caused him to throw up all the other children. Miraculously, they all lived. After ten years of war, Zeus banished Cronos and all the other Titans into the pit of Tartaros, a deep abyss and place of punishment. Eventually, Zeus released Cronos and made him king of the Elysian Islands, the home of the dead.

Cronos reminds you that what goes around comes around. If you want to create a bountiful life, it is best to do that with an open heart and a giving spirit. Cronos is an incredibly creative and powerful being. When you use that energy in harmony with your highest good, amazing results will become apparent in your life. It is best not to ask Cronos what to do but rather just ask him to use his creative abilities to manifest what you want.

Lilith

Associated Cultures

Sumerian / Hebrew

Lilith will help you

- Connect with your inner wisdom
- Have the courage to speak up for yourself
- Be playful and passionate
- Have incredible sex

Invocation

"Lilith, please allow me to see the world through the eyes of the creator. Help me to see the love in everything. Guide me and direct me. Show me how looking for evil limits my vision and stops me from experiencing my limitless nature."

Lilith was a Sumerian and Hebrew goddess, honored for her wisdom, freedom, courage, playfulness, passion, pleasure, and sexuality. During the time of the goddess, she was a powerful force for good, but at the dawn of patriarchy, she was portrayed as a demon by Levite priests. Once she was made into a demon, she was said to prey on women and children.

She was originally created to be the equal partner of Adam. Lilith refused to be subservient to him. Her attitude was a threat to the patriarch, so she was expelled from Eden and replaced with Eve, who was willing to be obedient. Prior to this, Lilith was the Great Mother who cared for the people and settled disputes with her gentle wisdom and powerful influence.

As a demon, she is blamed for seducing men in their sleep, causing nighttime emissions. She was also said to have sex with multiple partners and produce a hundred babies each day.

Lilith can be a goddess or a demon in your life. She can help you to see the wonder and magic of life or to see the underbelly of evil everywhere. Love or fear are your choices. Lilith knows that only the love is real and everything else is an illusion. She will help you embrace your divinity and see the love in everything. Lilith knows that either God exists or doesn't and knows beyond a shadow of a doubt the power of creation which infuses everything.

Shiva

Associated Culture

Hindu

Shiva will help you

- Live life passionately
- See the divine in everything
- Be happy, joyous, and free

- Energize your body and your life
- Harness the forces of nature
- Manifest your hopes and dreams

Invocation

If it's a rainy day and you'd like to see rainbows or sunshine, call upon Shiva. If you are tired, simply tap into the power of his dance. As the Lord of destruction, he can easily remove any obstacles in your path.

Shiva loves the sound of drums and the tinkling of bells, so use them to invite him into your life. By gently chanting his name, you can energize your body and profoundly change how you're feeling.

Shiva is the Hindu god of destruction. He is also known as Nataraja, the Lord of Dancers. In the Hindu tradition, dance induces trance and ecstasy and gives the dancer a direct experience with the divine. Shiva most often dances on his right foot, while his left foot is elegantly raised. His four arms represent the four cardinal directions. In his upper right hand, he holds an hourglass, the symbol of creation, beating with the pulse of the universe. In the palm of his upper left hand, he holds a flame, the symbol of destruction.

Shiva's second right hand is held in a gesture of protection. His other left hand crosses his body and points toward his uplifted foot, representing freedom from the cycle of birth and death. This hand is also held in a pose similar to an elephant's trunk, symbolizing Ganesha, Shiva's son and the remover of obstacles. His statue is often surrounded by a ring of fire. It stands on a lotus pedestal representative of the universal heart consciousness of each person.

Shiva's long and sensuous hair, his serene face, and his frenzied dancing are symbolic of the duality of the visible and invisible, of eternity and time. His serene tranquility reminds us of the joys of life, of the earth, of nature, of sex, and of the gifts of embracing a spiritual path. Shiva represents the archetypal aesthetic as well as the symbolic, passionate Dancer. He embodies the universal view in which the forces of nature and the hopes and dreams of man are blended together.

Demeter

Associated Culture

Greek

Demeter will help you

- Recover from the loss of a loved one, especially a child
- Adopt or conceive a child
- Connect with the seasons
- Find a lost child
- Increase your abundance

Invocation

Demeter loves the golden color of ripened wheat. To ask for her assistance, light a gold candle or place a sheaf of wheat on your altar. Allow yourself to feel her loving presence in your life, and she will be there. Write down your request on a piece of paper and read it to her. If it feels appropriate, ignite the paper with the candle.

Demeter is the earth goddess who brings forth the fruits of the earth. She is most closely associated with golden shafts of wheat and other grains. You can really feel her presence in the sun reflected off a field of golden, ripe wheat. She taught mankind all about farming so they could stop being nomads and settle down. Demeter is also thought of as the goddess of society. She is the fertility goddess and is very popular in rural, farming communities.

Demeter was the mother of Persephone, who was abducted by Hades, lord of the underworld. She wandered the Earth in search of her lost child, and while she sought her daughter, the earth failed to produce any crops.

Zeus ordered Hermes to rescue her. Before Persephone left, Hades gave her a pomegranate, which is a fertility symbol. When she ate of it, she was tricked into spending one-third of the year with him in the underworld. Hence the ebb and flow of the seasons began. The earth gives fruit only during the months when Persephone is with her mother. Thus, Demeter is associated with life and death, summer and winter.

In ancient art Demeter was often portrayed with a sheaf of wheat or sitting solemnly wearing a wreath of braided ears of corn. She shares the love of her daughter with all women and helps women overcome the profound grief experienced because of the loss of a child.

Kawailani Kapu

Associated Culture

Hawaiian

Kawailani Kapu will help you

- Let go of your fears
- Release anger
- Let go of stress

- Attract abundance
- Transform your greatest limitation into blessings

Invocation

Kawailani Kapu is a very open and loving goddess. Ask for her help and know she will be there. Light a candle and place it next to a glass of water. Look into the water and see her love reflected there.

Kawailani Kapu is the sacred goddess of fresh water. She brings life to the earth and sustenance to the people of Hawaii. Without water, the land shrivels up and dies. She is the life giver. Your body is up to 80 percent water, so she flows within each and every cell in your body. Water is an incredible element. If you try to hold water in your hand, it flows through your fingers. Water can change form depending on the temperature. It can be a liquid or solid or gas. It flows gently over any surface, yet it can create huge canyons over time. You will die without water.

As the water cascades over the numerous waterfalls in Hawaii, there are often rainbows. In the Puna district of the Big Island, there is a place of great healing where Pele, the goddess of fire, Kawailani Kapu, and her sister Namahao Ke Ka'i, the goddess of the ocean, come together and create a wonderful warm pond of healing and regeneration. It is the only place where the three sisters come together in peace and don't fight with one another. It is an incredible place to float and be supported by their power and strength.

Next time you watch the rain fall from the sky or stand next to a babbling brook or raging river, think of Kawailani Kapu. She blesses the water with her wisdom and loving strength. She will remind you of the magic and wonder life holds. She will ask you to let go of your anger and surrender to the love that always surrounds you.

Pachamama

Associated Culture

Peruvian

Pachamama will help you

- Fully savor your life
- Create blessings for yourself and others
- Attract abundance
- See the divinity in everything and everyone

Invocation

Your connection with Pachamama can happen anywhere. It can happen in the middle of a city, in your backyard, or in the middle of the jungle. The only thing necessary is your willingness and the desire to connect. Take a deep breath and feel the ground under your feet, give thanks for her presence, and ask for her guidance. Then take a few minutes each day to simply notice the world around you.

Pachamama is the great Earth goddess. She is seen as a huge dragon who lives beneath the mountains. Occasionally she quivers, and the earth shakes. She can send earthquakes to any place on the planet. The people see the mountains as her breast and the rivers as the milk of her love. Pachamama is worshipped as the beauty of a freshly tilled field. The people honor her with cornmeal and prayers before planting to ensure a good harvest. When people forget to honor her, she wakes them up with her earthquakes.

She is the goddess of fertility. Women perform daily rituals to honor her and guarantee they will have an adequate supply of food. Pachamama is the goddess of love and wants you to remember your divine nature. It saddens her to see people forgetting their connection to and dependence on nature. Without fertile soil and clean water, you won't have food to eat or water to drink. When was the last time you walked barefoot in the grass or stood out in the rain and gave thanks for the healing waters? Do you thank the Earth for supporting you? Do you feel your connection with the living entity called the Earth, or is the Earth just the lifeless planet you live on?

Pachamama invites you to connect and to remember. Feel the warmth of the sun on your face, allow the wind to embrace you, and think about where that wind came from. Next time you eat some food, allow yourself to see and to feel the stars and the moon with each bite. Think about all the people who made that meal possible, including nature and the farmer and the truck drivers and the grocery clerks and the spirit of the food itself.

Isis

Egyptian

Isis will help you

- Connect with the divine feminine
- Deepen your capacity to be intimate
- Remember your true self
- Enhance your creativity
- Joyously embrace life
- Master magic
- Ease childbirth

Invocation

To call upon Isis, wait until after dark and put on your favorite perfume or aftershave. When you ask for her help, you are likely to feel her lovingly enfold you in her winged arms. She is also considered the light bearer of heaven. A beautiful bowl of water with a floating candle is a wonderful backdrop for any request. When asking Isis for her assistance, say, "Isis, please teach me how to harness the incredible power of love. Give me the courage to make my choices lovingly, and fill me with the power of your hope. I give thanks for your presence in my life, for your love, your protection, and your wisdom."

Isis is the Egyptian winged goddess of the moon. From her inception she loved humans and taught women how to tame men enough to live with them and how to give birth safely.

Legend has it that Isis was married to Osiris. His brother Seth killed him and had his body cut into hundreds of pieces, which were scattered all over the land. Isis so loved Osiris that she gathered up all of his pieces and blew life back into his body. She loved Osiris so much that she re-membered him and in doing so reminds us to embrace all of the fragmented pieces of our psyche and spirit. Her invitation to each of us is to love ourselves enough to breathe life back into our own wholeness or holiness.

In another story, she tricked the god Ra into revealing his most secret name by making a deadly serpent out of dust and causing it to bite him. When Ra was at the point of death, he revealed his secret name, and she used the power of her words to heal him. Isis was then given the gift of great magic and the knowledge of how to use sound to manifest anything.

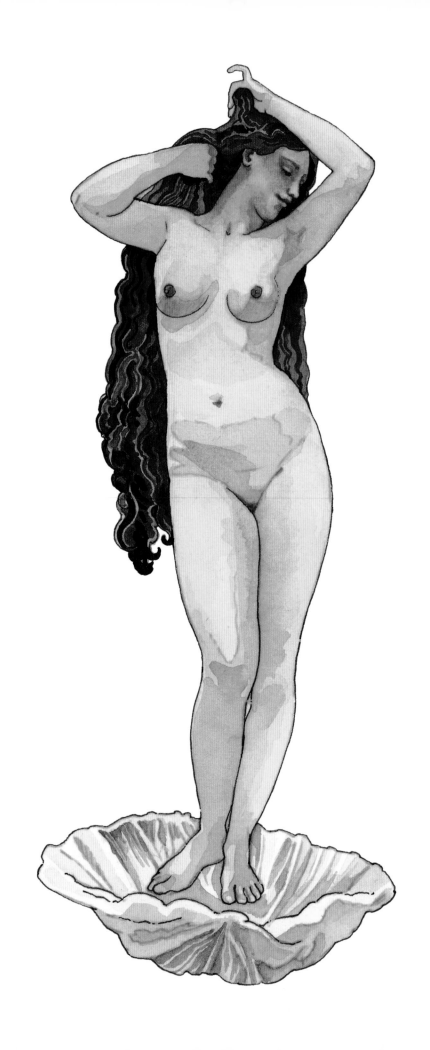

Venus

Associated Culture

Roman

Venus will help you

- Feel beautiful
- Find love
- Enhance any sexual encounter
- Buy the perfect outfit or find a great home
- Create abundance
- Discover your sense of style

Invocation

Venus loved looking at herself in a mirror, so call upon her by looking into a large mirror. Look lovingly at yourself and ask Venus to embrace you and fill you with a sense of pleasure and warmth. Ask her to help you remember the divine being you truly are and to help you with your challenges.

Venus was originally the goddess of gardens, vegetation, and vineyards. She became the goddess of love, beauty, and sexual passion. Venus is also the goddess of motherhood and marriage. She can influence our sense of style, an appreciation of art and culture, and each person's unique approach to romance. Venus governs sexual attraction and those who will find you attractive. Venus can also govern your attitudes toward finances and material possessions.

Venus is perhaps the most famous and honored goddess of the heart. When a woman embraces Venus's energy, it is difficult *not* to walk with a sassy step and rolling hips, pouring love forth from the eyes. Venus tells of fertility, love, and pleasure. Venus herself wasn't conceived from pleasure, but she worked hard to find her own happiness and joy. Venus married and bore children but concentrated almost completely on her extramarital affairs. Her many lovers included Aries, the god of war, and the handsome Adonis.

Venus loved to pamper herself and to cultivate her beauty. Truly, Venus has become the symbol for the essence of femininity. She will ask you to take the time to pamper yourself. Whether you are a man or a woman, she knows true happiness occurs only after you learn to love yourself unconditionally.

Hiranyagarbha

Associated Culture

Hindu

Hiranyagarbha will help you

- Find creative solutions
- Transform painful emotional traumas
- See the blessings in everything
- Successfully launch new projects
- Bring the light of love into even the darkest hours

Invocation

When you want to work with Hiranyagarbha, begin by meditating. Imagine yourself floating in the formless sea of creation. Allow yourself to get comfortable, and simply float without purpose or direction. Let yourself surrender to the nothingness and then ask for Hiranyagarbha's assistance.

Hiranyagarbha means "the golden womb from which the entire universe sprang forth." In one myth, Hiranyagarbha floated in a sea of nothingness, emptiness, and darkness for a year. Hiranyagarbha experienced nonexistence for the entire year and at the end of that time broke into two halves. One half was Swarga, which means "heaven," and the other half was Prithvi, which refers to earth. Brahma was born from Hiranyagarbha.

In some myths Hiranyagarbha is characterized as a single egg, and when Prana (spirit) combines with Bhuta (inactive matter) the universe is created. The single egg represents the feminine principle, which when combined with the male aspect becomes the Golden Egg, the life-bearing egg of creation.

Hiranyagarbha represents the incredibly limitless possibilities life holds. In the primordial darkness all possibilities exist, and it is from that darkness that the glorious light originates. It is often in a time of great darkness that the most profound personal growth takes place. Hiranyagarbha is the energy of creation personified, so call on him when you want to start a new project or end one that is no longer working for you. He is the embodiment of a nurturing, loving mother and a supportive father. He represents the inner and outer dimensions as well as the intuitive feminine and the action-oriented masculine aspect.

Tiamat

Associated Culture

Babylonian

Tiamat will help you

- Learn how to make choices
- Release your anger
- See events with greater clarity
- Expand your ability to love

Invocation

Find a deep purple candle and light it each evening. Call upon Tiamat and ask her to guide your thoughts and feelings. Invite her into your dreams. Know she will touch your mind, your heart, and your feelings. Pay attention to your dreams. Be sure you follow the guidance you receive.

Tiamat is the sea personified as a goddess. She is a monstrous embodiment of primordial chaos. Tiamat came forth from chaos and gives rise to the beauty and wonder of the universe. She is the primordial mother of all that exists, including the gods themselves.

The goddess Tiamat is an ancient and secretive deity of Babylonian descent. As the daughter of chaos and the mother of all matter, she fiercely defends her creations. Tiamat guards her wayward creation, human beings, even though at times they are destructive and hateful.

Tiamat was divided in two by one of the deities she birthed. One half of her body became heaven and the other half earth. Her eyes became the stars. She watches over all of creation.

Tiamat can show you how to move beyond angry impulses to engage the powerful forces of love and acceptance in your life. When you are in doubt about what to do next, call on Tiamat. From her lofty perspective she can see more clearly than you, so ask for her assistance and trust her guidance.

Mary

Associated Culture

Christian

Mary will help you

- Set yourself free
- Find love
- Forgive yourself and others
- Improve your health

- Let go of addictions
- Create a loving family
- Conceive a child
- Find a lost pet

Invocation

Light a candle and ask for Mary's loving guidance. Imagine all the millions of mothers throughout the world and all the women through the millennia who have cared for children. Allow yourself to align with that energy of the divine mother and ask for her guidance, love, and support.

During the second century, a movement arose to worship Mary as a goddess. Its members were called collyridians because of their practice of offering cakes, a practice started by people worshipping the Queen of Heaven. During the early days of Christianity, the goddess was still worshipped in many parts of the world. The church used Mary to convert those who revered the goddess. So is Mary a stereotype, or was she a goddess in her own right?

Mary was told by angels she was to give birth to the son of God. The Mother Goddess entered Mary of Nazareth's body so she could give birth to the masculine aspect of God. When the gods and goddesses come to Earth as humans, they get things done!

Mary fills the role of Sacred Feminine and allows you to identify with a goddess in a personal manner. She provides a loving female role model to strive for. Mary will show you how to connect with your divinity and to remember the balance you find there. When you enter this sacred space, you become part of Mary, and she will help you give birth to your sacred self.

Mary openly shares her love with you and will gladly show you how to love unconditionally. Her gentleness and passionate love of spirit will profoundly touch you. She will invite you to remember your own godlike nature and show you how to open your heart and mind to the magic and miracles that are part of your divine nature.

Bacchus

Associated Culture

Roman

Bacchus will help you

- Renew a relationship
- Transform your life
- Heal your body
- Savor the moment

Invocation

Pour yourself a glass of fine wine and toast Bacchus. Ask him for his assistance in your everyday life and the appearance of his wisdom. When you are going through a time of transition, ask him to help you use the energy of rebirth to govern your choices.

Bacchus was the god of wine and vegetation. He is also the lawgiver, in charge of civilization and a lover of peace. As the god of wine, he represents not only the intoxicating power of wine but also the deeper social ramifications of fine wines. He has a wonderful pallet and is able to teach you how to enjoy the finer things in life.

Bacchus dies every winter only to be reborn in the spring. This cyclical renewal reflects the seasonal nature of the Earth and holds within it the promise of rebirth for humans as well. The festivals celebrating his reappear-ance evolved into dramatic competitions and were a time of inner reflection as well as intoxicated orgies of carefree abandon.

His familiarity with the cycle of life and death gave him a working familiarity with the release and regeneration of the human soul. Bacchus will help a person transition painlessly from the earth plane. He will also help you embrace the gifts of life while not becoming attached to them. He will show you how to wear your earthly body lightly and fully savor the experience while avoiding the pitfalls of self-sabotage and ill health.

Neptune

Associated Culture

Roman

Neptune will help you

- Find lost objects
- Attract abundance
- Expand your vision about what is possible

- Let go of people, places, and things that no longer serve you
- Bring a feeling of safety and love into your life

Invocation

Neptune is a man of the sea. If you can, walk along the sea coast. Enjoy the smell of the salt air, feel the sand on your feet, and watch for the gifts the water brings you. If you can't get to the ocean, place some seashells in a bowl of salt water and ask Neptune for his guidance. You may hear a quiet chuckle as he reaches out to you.

Neptune is the god of the sea. He is usually depicted as a bearded, powerfully built man in the prime of his life. He usually carries a three-pronged trident in his left hand. He is a jocular man with a deep and resonant laugh. Being the god of the ocean, he is also associated with the energy of abundance. The ocean is rich in marine life and sustains the earth with its bounty. Neptune is surrounded with the riches and the wisdom of the sea.

Whales and dolphins are the keepers of ancient wisdoms. They help humans maintain balance and harmony in their lives and are the companions of Neptune. The ocean is a place of healing and profound riches. It is symbolic of the multidimensional nature of your being. Looking at the surface of the ocean, it looks devoid of life. As soon as you look beneath the surface, though, you see its teeming life, which is incredibly beautiful and vibrantly alive. The colors of the sea's inhabitants and their varied shapes and sizes boggle the mind.

Neptune will remind you of the many layers of your psyche. Your spiritual dimensions are rich with wisdom and grace. What has been niggling at the edge of your consciousness? What have you been longing to have in your life, and what have you been wanting to get rid of? What riches have you denied yourself? How can you capture the magical essence of your being and set it free?

Tyche

Associated Culture

Greek

Tyche will help you

- Beat the odds, so call upon her when things seem hopeless
- Create abundance in all areas of life
- Make clear and beneficial choices
- Discover your heart's true desire

Invocation

Because the first set of dice were found in her temple, you can use them as a symbol of your request for Tyche to come to your aid. Focus your thoughts on her, send out a deep sense of gratitude, and open your heart to her assistance.

Tyche is the Greek goddess of fortune, chance, and prosperity. She is the daughter of Zeus and was said to be quite irresponsible. She preferred to run around juggling a ball rather than to carry the Cornucopia filled with golden fruit. The first set of dice was found in Tyche's temple. They were thought to be symbolic of the capriciousness of life and the fickle manner in which Tyche decided the fortunes of mortals.

As the goddess of fortune, she is also associated with the growth of the spiritual, physical, and mental selves of all human beings. On the physical plane she may represent good fortune or bad luck, but symbolically she is a goddess of ancient wisdoms and spiritual growth. She is the rudder of destiny, which is influenced by our choices in life and the degree to which we are conscious of our connection with spirit. Tyche was very popular in ancient Greece. Several Greek cities chose her as their protector.

Tyche can show you how to beat the odds. As the goddess of prosperity, she can show you how to create great wealth and how to attract love and abundance into all areas of your life. She will remind you that life isn't really a crapshoot but a series of choices and outcomes. From experience you already know that love and gratitude will yield much better results than self-centered and heartless demands.

The Grandmother

Associated Culture

Native American

The Grandmother will help you

- Nurture yourself
- Create a loving home
- Find a lost child or pet
- Create a future filled with magic and miracles
- Connect with your inner wisdom at a profound level

Invocation

The Grandmother loves the wind, so step outside and feel the wind on your skin. Explain to the Grandmother the situation you would like her help with. Speak forth your request and imagine your words flying away in the wind. She will always answer you. You may get your answers in your dreams or on a billboard. Just be open to her guidance and know she will move heaven and earth to help you manifest your dreams.

The Grandmother is the ultimate Earth mother. She has been around for eternity and will continue to exist long after time has faded away into the nothingness from which it came. She has a huge heart and an incredible ability to see into the future. The Grandmother holds all the wisdom of the ages and has a profound understanding of how the universe operates. She loves sharing her wisdom and showing all of her children how to learn from her wisdom rather than having to learn through pain and suffering.

The Grandmother has the ability to reach deep into your soul and see your deepest dreams and desires. She can see your greatest good and knows what will help you enhance your spiritual growth so you can transform your life most efficiently. She knows what will make you truly happy and what will cause you suffering. Trust her guidance and her wisdom. If you ask for a relationship and instead find yourself alone, trust her. Focus on healing your relationship with yourself. If you ask for something and it doesn't appear the way you think it should, know she is thinking only of your long-term happiness.

The Grandmother is a wonderful resource and will assist you in healing your life and creating a profound and lasting connection with your spirit.

Wakan Tanka

Associated Culture

Lakota

Wakan Tanka will help you

- Connect with all of nature
- Feel the love which always surrounds you
- Enhance your creativity
- Cope with life in a loving and harmonious manner

Invocation

Music is a wonderful vehicle for prayer. It is said that Wakan Tanka always answers a prayer when he hears drums and rattles. Wakan Tanka is always available and listening to the prayers of his children. So ask with your heart and know your requests have already been answered.

In the Lakota tradition, "Wakan" is the name for their gods in general. Every creature and each object has its own *waken*, spirit without limitation. Wakan Tanka is "the great mystery" and the Supreme Being and creator of the Lakota Sioux. He is similar to supreme beings in the myths of many other North American peoples. Before creation, Wakan Tanka existed in a great emptiness called Han, which means darkness. Feeling lonely, he created companions for himself. First, he focused his energy and created the first god, Inyan (rock). Next, he used Inyan to create Maka (earth) and then combined them to produce Skan (sky). Skan brought forth Wi (the sun) from Inyan, Maka, and himself. Each of these four gods is separate and very powerful, but they are all still only a part of Wakan Tanka.

Wakan Tanka is the great mystery. He is all that is and all that will ever be. He is the alpha and the omega, with no beginning and no end. He has always existed and will always be. Anything that is born must die. But the spirit is not born; it is given, therefore it never dies. The spirit is awake, it is holy, always whole and complete.

Wakan Tanka is the source. He is the creator and he is the gateway to the beginning and to the end of your search. He reminds you that it is only within the source of your being that you find true happiness. Wakan Tanka speaks to you in every moment. All you need to do is open your heart and listen.

Shakti

Associated Culture

Hindu

Shakti will help you

- Find a fulfilling career
- Create abundance
- Get pregnant
- Understand your life's purpose
- Connect with your divine feminine

Invocation

Invoking the power of Shakti allows you to connect with the incredible power of limitless Creation. Since she is the personification of the divine feminine, when you call upon her, you'll immediately be surrounded by a feeling of warmth, acceptance, and love. Imagine all of your requests arriving into your life in a divinely magical way.

A beautiful way to call upon her is to fill a nice bowl with salt water and float some flowers and perhaps a floating candle on the surface. Gaze gently into the water and ask for her assistance. You could say: "Shakti, divine mother of us all, help me manifest the abundance and joy that is my birthright. Help me see you through your eyes of love rather than through my eyes of judgment and fear. I give thanks for all your blessings."

Shakti means the power and force of feminine energy. She represents the fundamental creative force underlying the cosmos and is the energizing power behind all of divinity. The whole universe is a manifestation of Shakti. She is a multidimensional goddess with many names, numerous personalities, and many different aspects. She is worshipped by millions of people in India and is often thought to be more important than the god Shiva himself.

Shakti represents the dynamic, creative, and proactive principles of feminine power. Lakshmi is one of her common representations. She is the Hindu goddess of wealth, light, wisdom, fortune, luck, beauty, courage, and fertility. She is called "the daughter of the sea" and is often pictured as a beautiful young woman standing in the center of a fully opened lotus flower.

Krishna

Associated Culture

Hindu

Krishna will help you

- Strengthen your relationships
- Create harmony
- Find your soul mate
- Bless your home
- Experience joy
- Overcome prejudice and judgment
- Fill your life with abundance

Invocation

If you allow yourself to step into the world of Hindu gods and goddesses, your life will take on a depth previously unavailable. The essence of the Hindu gods and goddesses is reflected in the beautiful artwork and sculptures that represent them. Open your heart to the grace, abundance, wisdom, and joy Krishna will bring you. To call upon him, light a candle, perhaps play some flute music, and ask for his assistance.

Krishna loves to play the flute and is the messenger of peace and laughter. He is usually depicted as a young prince. For centuries, children in India have been entertained by the stories of Little Krishna. These stories speak of the value of kindness, the importance of preserving what you create, and the boundless nature of wisdom.

Krishna is the eighth divine incarnation of the god Vishnu. In his youth, he loved to seduce the young maidens of his village. He was a hero, a warrior, and a teacher. As a youth, he lived in the country and spent a great deal of time herding animals in the pastures. He is the embodiment of love, and his joy is so divine that it overcomes all pain and suffering.

The love story between Krishna and the young maiden Radha is often portrayed as a quest for union with the divine. They grew up together; they played, danced, and wanted to be together forever. When Krishna left to safeguard the virtues of truth, she waited for him. The connection with Krishna is incomplete without his divine partner Radha.

Krishna's main message is one of harmony. He brings divine knowledge of the sacred realm to all people, with humility and acceptance for all paths. Krishna blesses everyone with his love. In the process, he destroys the darkness created by ignorance, prejudice, and judgment. Through his passion, he teaches about self-control and purity. Krishna believed that love was the greatest power in the universe and could overcome any obstacle.

Altjira

Associated Culture

Australian

Altjira will help you

- Work with your dreams
- Manifest your deepest desires
- Play and enjoy life
- Connect with the spiritual realms

Invocation

Clearly write down your hopes, dreams, and desires. Read them over just before you go to sleep and then ask Altjira to help you. In the morning, write down the dreams you had that night. He will send you messages and guidance. If you aren't sure what your dreams mean, ask him again the following night. He will work closely with you as long as you are willing. You spend a third of your life sleeping, and he is a powerful teacher of the dreamtime.

Altjira is the sky father of the Aranda tribes in central Australia. He is the god who created the Earth; he then retired to the top of the sky and became indifferent to mankind. He has the feet of an emu, and his wife and children have dog paws as feet. Strange feet are common for spirits or ancestors in Aboriginal beliefs. His name is also connected with the word meaning "to dream." In Aboriginal beliefs, there are two kinds of reality. One is everyday linear, objective activity. The other is the dreamtime, which is part of the limitless and expansive spiritual realms. Aborigines view dreamtime as more real than waking reality. The values and laws of Aboriginal society are established by the dreamtime. The dreamtime is a place filled with unusual spiritual powers.

Altjira is a wonderful ally. He may have retreated after he created the world, but he is still willing to help anyone who asks and is willing to work with the dreamtime. Despite his odd looks and aloof attitude, he loves being helpful. He reminds mortals how fluid physical reality is and invites them to use their creative instincts to transform their lives.

Altjira was able to bring the universe into existence by dreaming it. He will ask you what your dreams are and invite you to bring them into fruition in your life. Altjira knows that once you have the desire, creation is just a choice, and he will help you make the right choices.

Oshun

Associated Culture

African

Oshun will help you

- Have a child
- See the good in everything
- Lower your blood pressure
- Find diplomatic solutions
- Enhance your relationships
- Deepen your sexual satisfaction and expand your sensuality
- Attract lots and lots of money

Invocation

Oshun loves vivid colors. Write down your request and wrap it in a colorful scarf or light a bunch of bright-colored candles. Sit quietly and watch the sunset while you allow yourself to connect with this beautiful and powerful woman. Her smile can light up the world. Her laughter soothes even the most savage breast. Once you ask Oshun for her help and connect with her, you have a friend for life.

Oshun is the Yoruba goddess of love and pleasure, beauty, and sensuality. She will show you how to use diplomacy. She is also often associated with money. Oshun teaches people how to overcome difficulties through kindness and negotiation. She is a very generous goddess, but due to her ferocious temper, she is also feared. Her mood can change in a moment from a balmy summer day into a tumultuous raging storm. But after the storm, she brings forth her brilliant rainbows.

Oshun is depicted wearing seven bracelets and a mirror on her belt. She carries river water in her pot and is accompanied by her cricket and peacock. At times she appears as an old woman who is sad about the loss of her youth. At other times she is a beautiful, tall, brown-skinned woman totally comfortable with her sexuality. She is a woman of mystery and is well acquainted with the ancient mystical secrets and witchcraft.

If she's caught your attention, she has much to teach you. Originally she was a river goddess, so Oshun will teach you how to successfully navigate your life. She will show you how to run the rapids without getting wet. Her skillful diplomacy will help you get a raise at work or communicate more clearly with a loved one.

Lakshmi

Lakshmi will help you

- Find creative solutions
- Create abundance
- Discover the perfect career
- Procure a fabulous place to live
- Connect with the love of your life

Invocation

Lakshmi adores the color pink. If you can find a pink lotus flower, float it in a bowl of water, or find a floating pink candle and light that instead. Say a blessing and then ask for her help. Just explain the problem and ask for her guidance to find a solution.

Lakshmi is a Hindu goddess who represents abundance, prosperity, and wealth. She was known as the Mother Earth Goddess who arose from the primordial sea of milk often found in Hindu legends. She is often depicted as a beautiful golden brown woman with four arms. Generally she is shown resting on a lotus flower. As the consort of Vishnu, she is often shown washing his feet as he sits on the thousand-headed serpent. She is the embodiment of the active female principle of Shakti in the male god.

Lakshmi will show you how to take definitive action when necessary and how to surrender and let go when that is the best course of action. Lakshmi is a wonderful teacher who brings balance into any situation. She knows how to relax and enjoy life, savoring every moment. She is always associated with the lotus flower, which is the symbol of spiritual growth and enlightenment.

When you call on Lakshmi, it is best to ask her guidance before you decide on a course of action. As the goddess of abundance, she will help you create plenty of whatever you want. She can help you create an abundance of trauma and drama as well as of happiness and joy, but when asked for her wisdom, she will always guide you toward joy.

Brahma

Associated Culture

Hindu

Brahma will help you

- Create anything
- Create abundance, happiness, love, and joy
- Transform your life
- Heal your mind, body, and soul

Invocation

Traditionally, people light incense in front of an image of Brahma when they want to enlist his aid. You can simply close your eyes and imagine yourself standing in front of this loving god of creation and ask for his assistance. Very clearly ask him to help create that which will be for your highest purpose and would bring you lasting happiness and joy.

Brahma is the creator of the universe, and everything, including all living beings, is said to have evolved from him. He is often depicted as being red with four heads and four arms. His heads face each of the four directions. One of his hands is held up in blessing. Since he is the god of knowledge, he holds a symbol of his great wisdom in another hand. In his other two hands he often holds a staff and water pot, which symbolizes abundance.

The world exists for one day in the life of Brahma, one kalpa. At the end of the day, the whole world is destroyed when Brahma goes to sleep for the night, which is of equal length to one kalpa. When he awakens, he once again creates the whole world. Brahma lives for one hundred years,

at which time the world dissolves back into its elemental nature. Another Brahma then begins the whole process over again.

Brahma's vehicle is a white swan or goose that has magical abilities. Among other things, it can separate good from evil. Unlike other Hindu gods, Brahma has no weapon. He also created seven sages to help him craft the universe.

Brahma is a loving god. He cares about all of his creations. He is part of the Hindu trinity along with Visnu and Siva. It is no error that he is called the god of creation. He will help you create whatever you want if you just ask for his assistance.

Vakarinė

Vakarinė will help you

- Find your way in life
- Feel nurtured and loved
- See the beauty in everything
- Be grateful for your life

- Arrive on time
- Feel renewed and refreshed
- Heal your mind, body, and spirit

Invocation

Go outside and look at the evening sky. Watch the stars as they twinkle and move across the heavens. Allow yourself to feel your connection to the universe. Then ask Vakarinė to help you. She will embrace and care for you as she has cared for Saulė all these millennia.

Saulė (the Sun) is the beautiful goddess of the sky who lives in a palace far to the east. Every morning she rides across the sky in a brilliant chariot made of gold, copper, or fire and pulled by two white horses. In the evening, after the chariot sinks into the Baltic Sea, Saulė rides a golden boat across the waters. The boat is steered by the goddess Perkūnėlė, who nurtures and bathes the tired and dusty Saulė. She sees her on her way the next morning, refreshed and renewed, shining and ready for a new journey through the sky.

Saulė's husband was Mėnulis, a young god of the moon who dressed in silver attire. He was the guardian of night and time. Deep, rich mythological imagery was associated with the four phases of the Moon, each one of vital importance to animals, plants, and the weather. In one tale, solar eclipses are explained as the Sun and the Moon kissing each other.

Vakarinė was the goddess of the Evening Star who made the bed for Saulė each night. With her golden hair and an image of the Sun on her crown, she was a maiden of remarkable beauty. She wore a mantle of stars secured with a moon-shaped brooch on her shoulder and was often considered to be more beautiful than the Sun.

Vakarinė will show you how to nurture yourself as you move through your life. She will help you know your own value and remember that without you, the universe would be incomplete.

Hina

Associated Culture

Hawaiian

Hina will help you

- Create more passion in your life
- Connect with your spiritual nature
- Make your menses more regular and less painful
- Attract more abundance
- See the magic and wonder in all of life

Invocation

Go outside and spend some time basking in the moonlight. Allow yourself to connect with her gentle, loving energy. Open your heart and your mind so you can be enfolded with the magical energy of the night and imagine your dreams gliding effortlessly on the moonbeams.

Hawaiians know that words carry a great deal of power and that they are how we create our reality. So choose your words well, and make sure you ask for what you do want instead of what you don't want. The universe doesn't hear the "not" part, so if you say "I don't want to struggle," what you are really asking for is more opportunities to struggle.

Hina is the goddess of love and peace, renewal and creativity. In Hawaiian chants there are many goddesses named Hina, each playing a slightly different role. There is Hinapukui`a, the goddess of fishermen, and Hina`opuhalako`a, who gave birth to the reefs and the teeming life they contain. There is also the Hina who holds sway over the sacred art of making kapa (a fabric made of beaten mulberry bark that was used primarily for clothing), and there is the Hina who is goddess of the moon and stars.

Hina is a powerful and pervasive presence in Hawaiian mythology. She is an incredibly passionate and humble goddess who has great love for human beings and for the aina (land). As the goddess of the moon, she rules over the tides of life as well as the ocean. She is keeper of the heavens and her greatest gift is guidance. She will help you connect with your inner wisdom and intuition. As the keeper of the tides, she also has dominion over the blood flows of women. She brings gentle rhythmic patterns to the world and life in general.

Apollo

Associated Culture

Greek

Apollo will help you

- Substantially enhance your creativity
- Bring passion to everything you do
- See the world from an expansive perspective
- Increase your psychic abilities

Invocation

Apollo loves working with humans, so simply call upon him. Laurel leaves have a wonderful scent and are useful for preserving food. Gather some and sprinkle them around your bed. The aroma will help you feel the presence of Apollo as you sleep. He is an elegant god who stirs the creative heart and passions. Pay attention to your dreams and make note of the messages Apollo brings you.

Apollo is the god of prophecy, a patron to musicians and poets. He is also the leader of the Muses. He is often shown holding a lyre or kithara, which are symbolic of the sound that brought forth the universe; he wields the energy of creation. Apollo has dominion over healing, light, medicine, poetry, the intellect, dance, prophecy, shamans, and all forms of creativity. Besides the oracle in Delphi, he had other notable ones in Clarus and Branchidae.

Those who want to invoke the guidance of Apollo often use the laurel leaf. Animals that were considered sacred attributes of him are the wolf, swan, hawk, raven, crow, snake, mouse, grasshopper, and the mythical griffin (a mixture of the eagle and the lion). The swan and grasshopper are symbolic of music and song, while the hawk, raven, crow, and snake are most useful when aligning with divination. Apollo is believed to have control over plagues, so he was often called upon during epidemics.

At a profound level, Apollo represents harmony and balance, order and reason. He has a deep love for humans. In the capacity of a muse, he will inspire you to live a life that is in alignment with your highest purpose. Apollo will help you cut through the illusionary nature of reality and connect with a reality that is rich and rewarding.

Quetzalcoatl

Associated Culture

Aztec

Quetzalcoatl will help you

- Transform problematic situations
- Alter time so you can accomplish the impossible
- Bring abundance into your life in surprising ways
- Let go of the past
- Remember to be in the moment

Invocation

Quetzalcoatl is often shown moving and dancing with his feathered headdress. One way to call upon him is with movement. Begin to rhythmically move and sway until you can feel the power of creation flowing through you. Another way to invoke him is to shout your wishes into the wind.

Quetzalcoatl is called the feathered snake god. He is the creator, the sky god who organized the original cosmos and has participated in the endless cycle of creation and destruction of the various human civilizations. This is considered the fifth humanity to inhabit this planet. Quetzalcoatl descended into the underworld and gathered the bones of humans from early epochs. He sprinkled his blood on the bones and brought the current race of humans to life. Quetzalcoatl is also the god of the wind, the water god, and the god of fertility. He brought maize to the people, showed them how to cultivate, introduced agriculture, and gave them the calendar. He also guides artisans.

Quetzalcoatl was an integral part of everyday life. He was also described as light-skinned and bearded, and it was predicted he would return in a certain year. So when Cortez appeared in 1519, Montezuma was easily convinced Cortez was the returning god. Quetzalcoatl was worshipped in many places. A six-tiered pyramid is dedicated as a temple of Quetzalcoatl in Teotihuacán. Quetzalcoatl has the power to transform and create. As the god of wind, water, fertility, and creation, he has the ability to influence your life in a profound manner. As the feathered serpent, he brings you the gift of insights. He can show you where your thinking limits your experience of life and where it creates joy and abundance.

He is often represented as the morning star, a symbol of new beginnings. What would you like to start anew in your life? What seeds would you like to plant and what weeds would you like to see removed?

Danu

Danu will help you

- Get in touch with the childlike magic of life
- Play and enjoy even life's most arduous tasks

- Bring more joy into your relationships
- Find a lost pet
- Make your garden flourish

Invocation

Go out in the twilight and call her name. You may see sparkles of light or feel the wind suddenly rise. Send out your hopes and prayers on the wings of the wind and know Danu has the ability to weave magical spells on all of life.

Danu is the Celtic goddess of the wind. She is the matriarch of the gods, and Earth goddess of fertility, abundance, and protection. She is also the goddess of wisdom. Danu is the oldest of the Celtic goddesses. Her influence reached far and near and even spread to the British Isles and Europe, where the Danube River was named for her. Even though very few stories about Danu have survived, the reverence in which she was held still remains. When Christianity came to Ireland, it is said her followers retreated into the forest so they could maintain the old ways. Eventually, they became fairies, and her legend lives on in their hearts. She is most powerful in the twilight hours, and she excites the imagination of those who can see magic at that time of day.

Danu is very present in the lives of humanity today. People may not recognize her or know her story, but that doesn't stop her from being a very healing presence. So many people are enamored with fairies, and that is often how she presents herself—as a magical creature capable of doing amazing miracles.

Mukuru

Associated Culture

African

Mukuru will help you

- Tap into your compassionate nature
- Call rain during a drought
- Overcome grief
- Release the past
- Engage your sense of humor

Invocation

You don't need to do anything special to call upon Mukuru. Just ask, and he will be there for you. He has a big heart and a jovial laugh. Don't be surprised if it starts to rain shortly after you ask for his assistance.

Mukuru is the ancestral god and the god of creation of the Herero bushmen of Namibia.

He is very kind and generous of spirit and one of the most benevolent gods. He has no parents and was said to emerge from the omumborombonga tree. Mukuru is venerated as one of the "Old Ones." He is invoked often because Njambi, their supreme god, isn't available for the mundane matters of mere mortals. Mukuru, on the other hand, really cares about humans and is always available for guidance and assistance. He shows his love of the people by bringing life, healing the sick, and maintaining the ancient traditions. Rain is one of the most valuable commodities to the Herero bushmen, and he regularly brings the rains to the people.

The Herero believe their chief is the physical incarnation of Mukuru, and as such, he shares culture with the people. The Herero don't make offerings to Mukuru because he is such a loving god. Death is part of life, and they view it as being called home by god, so they aren't very upset by the process.

Mukuru is an imaginative god who comes up with creative solutions. He also has a sense of humor, so you may find yourself laughing unexpectedly when you invite him into your life. If you are still holding onto any old emotional wounds, you may find yourself having a long overdue cry.

Thor

Associated Culture

Norse

Thor will help you

- Dispel any illusions in your life
- Find love
- Heal your body by cleansing it on the cellular level
- Bring your behaviors and thoughts into balance
- Release addictions

Invocation

Light the largest candle you have and speak Thor's name loudly. Take a deep breath and loudly shout your request to him. Demand his presence in your life and watch as everything takes on a surreal quality. He will create magic and miracles if you let him.

Thor is the Norse god of thunder, storms, war, and justice. He is a son of Odin and was more popular than his father because Thor didn't demand human sacrifice. Thor was usually portrayed as a large, powerful man with a red beard and eyes of lightning. Despite his ferocious appearance, he is seen as a protector against the forces of evil for both gods and humans.

The Norse believed that during a thunderstorm, Thor rode through the heavens on his chariot pulled by goats. Lightning flashed when he threw his hammer. Just as the air smells fresh and clean after a thunderstorm, if you ask Thor into your life, you will feel cleaner and more vibrant than you did before. He will light up your life with his spirit and bring balance and harmony into your thinking. He is a powerful force of justice and right action in the world.

Thor may look like an angry god, but he is really quite benevolent and generous of spirit. When he roars into your life, you can be sure others will hear you speak and will listen to your opinions. He has the power to bind and unbind a person's thinking. He can show you how your thoughts affect your health and your life. He will show you how true justice serves everyone and how injustice affects the whole world.

Ganesha

Associated Culture

Hindu (India)

Ganesha will help you

- Remove obstacles
- Create abundance
- Succeed in artistic endeavors and writing projects

- Have more harmonious relationships
- Feel happier and have peace of mind
- Attain and maintain a deep spiritual connection

Invocation

Because Ganesha is the patron of writing, you can simply write him a letter requesting his assistance. Then light a piece of incense and burn the letter. He welcomes all requests and joyously helps all those who have an open heart and are willing to accept his aid. You might say something like: "Most beloved Ganesha, I welcome you into my life. May my heart be filled with your love and your laughter, and may I always be guided by your wisdom. Please remove any obstacles in my path and grant me the peace of mind to understand my journey and make choices that benefit myself and all others. I give thanks for your presence and your guidance. May laughter fill my days and joy enfold my heart. Thank you, Ganesha, for all your help."

Ganesha, the elephant-headed god, is extremely popular in India. He is the best known and most beloved representation of divinity in Hinduism. There are several stories about how he got his elephant head. In one, Ganesha was created directly by Shiva's laughter. When Shiva became concerned that Ganesha was too alluring, he gave Ganesha the head of an elephant and a protruding belly.

Ganesha is known as the god of obstacles. He can easily remove any obstacles in your path or place one in your path if he thinks you need to slow down. He is the god of intellect and his consorts are wisdom, prosperity, and attainment. Ganesha is affectionately honored at the beginning of any ritual or project and is called upon first in prayer. He will bring you peace of mind, success in undertakings, enlightenment, and intelligence. He is also known as the god of education, knowledge and wisdom, literature, and the fine arts. Ganesha is also the lord of light and hope. He is called a laughing god, so your chances are good that simply by calling upon him, you will feel better.

Hekate

Associated Culture

Greek/ Celtic

Hekate will help you

- Harness your mystical nature
- Influence your thinking
- Manifest your dreams
- Have an easy and pain-free childbirth
- Open up new possibilities
- Heal your wounded self

Invocation

On the night of the full moon, find a place out in nature where you can see the moon rising. As the moon rises, reach out toward the moon and call out Hekate's name. Explain the nature of your request and hold it in your heart as you watch the moon. When the moon is almost overhead, give thanks for Hekate's guidance and love and know that powerful magic has been released in your life.

Hekate is the goddess of the wilderness and child-birth. She is a goddess shrouded in mystery. She is the only goddess powerful enough to travel to all three worlds: heaven, earth, and the underworld. She is a powerful, action-oriented goddess. She is one of the original moon goddesses. Hekate is also associated with the mystical realms and magic. "Heka" means "magical speech" in Egyptian, while "Hekate" means "influence from afar" in Greek.

Hekate has played many roles throughout the ages. She has been called the one before the gate, the attendant who leads, the light bringer, the child nurse, and the mother of all living beings on the Earth. Her parentage is not clear, but her role as a powerful creative force is.

Hekate is a woman of mystery. She will invite you to go into the wilderness of your unconscious and clear out all of your old, outdated beliefs. She will bring the light of love to those places of darkness within your mind and your spirit. Freedom is the gift she offers if you are ready and willing to take it.

Zeus

Associated Culture

Greek

Zeus will help you

- Maintain the moral high road
- Find just solutions to disagreements in your life
- Prevail in legal issues
- Recover lost money
- Elect honest and supportive government officials

Invocation

Zeus is the regal ruler of Mount Olympus. If you ask for his help in legal matters, be certain you are on the right side of the law. Zeus is the defender of justice. Light a navy blue candle and explain your predicament. Ask Zeus to exert his powerful influence in your life. If the weather has been too stormy, ask Zeus to quiet the elements.

Zeus was the supreme ruler of Mount Olympus. He was considered the spiritual leader of all humans as well as the leader of the gods. He upheld the law and set the standard for morals and justice. Zeus was originally the weather god who controlled thunder and lightning, and he is often pictured holding a lightning bolt. Zeus was the protector of the Greek monarchy until Greece became a democracy. Then he became the lawgiver, the chief judge, and a consummate peacemaker. Zeus replaced violence with peace and became the champion of political freedom. His other duties included protecting supplicants, summoning people to the various festivals, and giving prophecies.

Zeus helped maintain balance and harmony in civilized life. He was considered the father of the gods and he was a loving father! He cared a great deal about humanity and takes his role as guardian of justice quite seriously. He is a wonderful arbitrator and will help you find harmonious solutions to even the most difficult situations. Zeus will also awaken you from your delusions about a situation, with a lightning bolt if all else fails. When you call on him, expect the unexpected.

Horus

Associated Culture

Egyptian

Horus will help you

- Make right any injustices
- Intuitively know the just thing to do
- Protect your home from intruders
- Stay safe while traveling

Invocation

Horus was associated with the sun god, so begin by facing the sun. Call his name and state your desires. He has a deep, resonant voice and he laughs often, so you may hear a chuckle as you explain your dilemma. Be open to his guidance and really allow yourself to feel his presence. He brings the incredible love of his beautiful mother everywhere he goes, so expect to hear her lyrical voice as well. He is an ancient god, so he has seen it all and is very creative with his solutions.

Horus is the falcon-headed god and is among the most important Egyptian gods. His mother is Isis, and he was magically conceived after his father, Osiris, was murdered by his uncle Seth. Isis reassembled Osiris because of her immense love for him. Horus eventually avenged his father's death.

The Pharaoh was considered the earthly incarnation of Horus. Because most pharaohs took the name Horus, eventually each region had its own version. It is nearly impossible to distinguish a "true" Horus from all these many different permutations. Eventually Horus became a general term for a great number of falcon gods, which were worshipped all over Egypt.

No matter which version of Horus you call upon, they were all just, loyal, and respectful gods. He was the ultimate role model for young men and the ideal of the dutiful son who grows into a man of integrity. Some viewed him as an avatar or enlightened being living here on Earth to help humanity live life to its fullest. The story of Horus and Seth symbolically represents Horus's desire and duty to keep the world safe from injustice and cruelty.

Horus will help you create balance in your life. He will show you how to fly over any of life's apparent obstacles and make choices that will bring joy and abundance effortlessly into your world.

Obàtálá

Associated Culture

African

Obàtálá will help you

- Connect with ancient sacred wisdoms
- Employ gratitude as a transformational tool
- Settle disputes fairly
- Understand and release limiting beliefs

Invocation

Carefully formulate your request, remembering that morality and fairness are qualities of Obàtálá's followers. When you are clear, light a white candle and ask for his assistance. He is a passionate man, and as long as you avoid drunkenness, he will move heaven and earth to help you.

Obàtálá is a Nigerian Yoruba god who created the universe. When Obàtálá makes each person, his father, Olorun, breathes life into his or her body and gives the person a soul. Obàtálá is one of the most important gods of the Nigerian Yoruba people. He is also the god of the north and is always dressed in white. His followers embody morality, fairness, and justice in their lives so that his robe remains unblemished. He is considered a deity of piety. The north is the place of knowledge, teaching, balance, abundance, sacred wisdom, thankfulness, finding one's inner treasures, intuition, trust, and spiritual alchemy. As the god of the north, Obàtálá encourages you to embrace its gifts.

When Obàtálá got drunk on palm wine, he created handicapped people and then he became their patron.

People born with congenital defects are called "eni orisa," which literally means "people of Obàtálá." He is a very loving and merciful god. He creates balance, peace, and harmony wherever he goes. When you want to breathe life into a new project or revitalize an old one, call on Obàtálá. If you are questioning someone's integrity, ask Obàtálá to help you see the truth. If you have a major decision to make in your life, he will help you find the most beneficial and harmonious solution. Wherever you need to access your intuition and embrace your inner treasures, Obàtálá will remind you of the gifts you already possess and teach you to use them.

Namahao Ke Ka'i

Associated Culture

Hawaiian

Namahao Ke Ka'i will help you

- Connect with an incredible power and wisdom
- Access the expansive energy of creation
- Attract abundance
- Feel nurtured and loved
- Manifest your wildest dreams

Invocation

Namahao Ke Ka'i is the goddess of the ocean, where all water began. Hold a glass of water and think about the beauty of this planet. Give thanks for its life-giving ability. Imagine filling the water with your love and gratitude. Speak forth your request and let Namahao Ke Ka'i into your heart and your mind. She never denies a heartfelt prayer, especially one filled with gratitude for already having received the gift.

Namahao Ke Ka'i is the goddess of the ocean who lovingly embraces the Hawaiian Islands. She has had a long-standing rivalry with her sister Pele. She demands respect and can easily swallow up a careless person. Very little is written about Namahao Ke Ka'i because the Hawaiian tradition is an oral tradition. But anyone who has stood at the edge of the ocean and been mesmerized by the waves has felt her presence. There are millions of words written about the mystery, magic, and illusive call of the sea. Those writers have all been inspired by Namahao Ke Ka'i. She is the source of great abundance and contains the wisdom of the ages.

An incredible number of different creatures live within her. She lovingly gives life to whales and dolphins, beautiful fish, incredible coral, and hundreds of other beings. If you've ever seen a video of a jellyfish propel itself through the water, you will have a sense of her graceful energy. If you stand by the shore and watch a storm swell hit the beach, you know how powerful she is. Namahao Ke Ka'i is a wonderful goddess to know.

Chicomecoatl

Associated Culture

Aztec

Chicomecoatl will help you

- Increase your abundance
- Create a home full of love and joy
- Have children
- Find a wonderful job
- Launch any creative endeavor

Invocation

If you are feeling lighthearted, make some popcorn and call upon Chicomecoatl. Explain your concerns to her and ask for her guidance. You could place a dried bunch of colored maize on your table and ask her to bless your home and your life.

Chicomecoatl is the Aztec goddess of maize. She is also called the goddess of nourishment and of abundance. Every September a young girl was sacrificed in her honor. Her symbol is an ear of corn, and she appears is several ways. Most often she appears as a young girl carrying water flowers or as a woman carrying the sun as a shield. At times, she is represented as a woman whose embrace means certain death. In art, she has lines on her red face, wears a large headdress, and has ears of corn on her back and in her hands.

Chicomecoatl represents the cycle of planting, harvesting, and replanting as well as the human cycle of birth, death, and rebirth. The Aztecs' lives revolved around maize because it was one of their main food sources. As a symbol, a single ear of corn has many kernels, each capable of propagating an abundance of new life. The girl sacrificed to Chicomecoatl was always the most beautiful girl in the village because of the reverence, love, and honor the people felt for their goddess of corn.

What areas of your life could use more love and attention? You don't have to sacrifice your wants and needs in order to feel loved. Call upon Chicomecoatl to show you how to bring forth the most amazing harvest of love, abundance, and delight in your life.

Ixchel

Associated Culture

Mayan

Ixchel will help you

- Heal a broken heart
- Give birth to a beautiful and healthy child
- Easily move through menopause
- Build a successful, happy, and abundant life

Invocation

Stand in the moonlight and allow yourself to feel her presence. Imagine yourself surrounded by her love. Speak forth your deepest wishes, hopes, and dreams. Ask her to help manifest a life befitting the god/goddess you are. She is an ancient goddess capable of profound healing. In calling upon her, you open yourself to a powerful healing force.

Ixchel is the Mayan goddess of the earth and moon and the patroness of pregnant women. Just as the moon has different phases, she has many different faces. Ixchel is a shape-shifter with a variety of different aspects, one for each phase of a person's life. As the crescent moon, she is the goddess of fertility and works with young women. As the waning moon, she is called the Grandmother and is associated with aging and the loss of fertility. As the Grandmother, she is the wise midwife who guides young women who are just beginning to start their families and build new lives.

Ixchel invented the art of weaving. She is also known as the rainbow goddess, who brings life-giving water to the thirsty land. Ixchel is the maiden and the crone and the keeper of the life cycle. She is the goddess of all souls, the protector of the newly born and the keeper of the bones and souls of the dead.

Ixchel will help you give birth to a happier and freer you. She will help you to transform anything. She has an incredibly loving heart and can touch the deepest core of your being to help you completely release the past. She reminds humans that it isn't necessary to carry the pain of the past. The past is just a memory, and the future has yet to spring forth into reality. Ixchel invites you to fill the present moment with joy so you will create a future filled with that joy.

Aine

Aine will help you

- Conceive a child
- Heal if you are a victim of abuse
- Stop sexual harassment
- Attract abundance and love
- Make your garden flourish
- Enforce vows

Invocation

If you can, wait until the full moon to call upon Aine. Go out in the moonlight and call her name. Ask for her help and allow the moonlight to fill your heart and your mind. Whisper your wishes into the wind and know that Aine will use her magic to make them happen.

Aine is the goddess of love and fertility. She is also known as the Fairy Queen of Munster. In some myths, she was a mortal woman but was tricked into becoming a goddess by a fairy who enchanted her. Aine liked humans and often slept with mortal men, which resulted in producing fairy children. Aine was the original Sun goddess and was also considered the Moon goddess.

As the goddess of the four powerful energies of earth, air, water, and fire, Aine is a force to be reckoned with. Midsummer night's eve is the day she is traditionally worshipped with torchlight processions through the fields.

Aine is one of the great goddesses of Ireland. She encourages human love and knows that it is one of the most powerful forces on this planet.

Aine knows all about magic, so she is a wonderful goddess to have on your side. She will show you how to create prosperity and abundance in all areas of your life. Aine makes sure all vows are kept. She will help you get rid of unsuitable mates and find loving ones and also help you reveal fairies. Her sacred animals are the hare and the swan. As the goddess of fertility, she has authority over crops and animals.

Sophia

Associated Culture

Greek

Sophia will help you

- Create prosperity
- Facilitate negotiations
- Find your soul mate
- Connect with all of your talents and gifts
- Dispel prejudice and ignorance

Invocation

Since Sophia is the mother of creation, the best time to call upon her is early in the morning. Get up just before dawn and watch the sunrise. Call upon her and ask her earnestly for her help. Breathe deeply into the core of your being and ask her to bless you with her wisdom and strength.

Sophia is the mother of creation and the goddess of all wisdom and fate. Her symbol, the dove, represents pure spirit. She is crowned by stars, indicating her absolute divinity. She is mentioned in many traditions and has many names, including the Black Goddess, Divine Feminine, and the Mother of God.

To the Gnostic Christians, she was the Mother of Creation and her consort was Jehovah. The goddess Sophia was the beginning, the source of wisdom, and the keeper of the knowledge of all that is righteous and just. When people honor her sound wisdom and guidance, rulers lead their kingdoms to prosperity. When her love and wisdom are ignored, darkness and ignorance thrive, the proverbial wasteland of foolishness eats away at the soul, and nations perish. Sophia was born in the silence of all wisdom. She gave birth to both the male and female. Together, they gave birth to the entire physical universe. When humans were created, Sophia loved them dearly with all her heart and mind.

With her gift of understanding, Sophia brings a deeper meaning to human experience. She knows that when you see the bigger picture, you find unexpected treasures. When you stand back and gain emotional distance, you can see even the most traumatic experiences as the birthplace of your most treasured strengths. Only in times of great stress are heroic feats truly appreciated.

Enki

Associated Culture

Sumerian (Iraq)

Enki will help you

- Bring order to your life
- Organize your home and office
- Feel inspired to create
- Attract abundance
- Throw an elegant party

Invocation

To call upon Enki, sit beside some running water or place a beautiful bowl of water on an indigo piece of cloth. Then say, "Enki, god of wisdom and order, I invite you to bring your sweet presence into my life. Please guide me and direct me. Bestow your wisdom and grace upon me and upon [explain your request]. I give thanks for your help."

Enki is the god of wisdom and sweet water. He is the god of creation, intellect, order, and civilization and is able to bring the dead back to life. He is usually described as a figure with a great horned headdress and tiered skirt with two streams of water originating from his shoulders. They represent the Tigris and Euphrates Rivers. At times, he carries a vase from which fresh fish are jumping. He may also hold a large eaglelike bird, symbolizing clouds rising up from the waters and feeding the land with their nourishing rain.

Enki is the source of all secret and magical knowledge about life and the gift of immortality. Enki possessed the secret of culture; he invented civilization; and he assigned each person his or her destiny. He created order in the cosmos and filled the rivers with fish. As father of all plants, he invented the plow and the yoke so that farmers could till the earth and grow their grain.

There is gentleness and warmth to this god of wisdom. Enki will gladly embrace you with his love, guide your thoughts, and give you visions of the endless possibilities life holds. He reminds humans that this world is a cornucopia of possibilities and that all limitations are self-imposed.

Ra

Associated Culture

Egyptian

Ra will help you

- Overcome depression
- Triumph over addictions
- Free yourself from an abusive relationship
- Free yourself from debt
- Live life to its fullest

Invocation

Ra is often shown holding the sun over his head like a large golden disc. Become quiet for a moment and imagine the sun directly over your head. Take a long, deep breath and ask Ra for his help. If you feel so inclined, light a yellow candle. Ra can help you overcome even the most stubborn addiction. Every time you feel the urge to indulge in your addiction, ask Ra to remove the desire and he will.

Ra was the most important of the Egyptian gods. He was symbolized by the sun when it was high in the sky and was worshipped throughout Egypt. Ra was the king of the gods and the father of creation. He commanded the chariot that carried the sun on its journey across the sky each day. As king of the gods, Ra was the benefactor of the pharaoh.

Ra was the only god, aside from Osiris, who is not on the Earth. Ra is an aging god, still very powerful, but no longer wanting to watch over his children. He has gone to the sky to watch over the world. Each day Ra travels across the sky in his chariot with the sun. At night he travels through the underworld, giving support to the dead while the great monster Apep tries to prevent the sun god from emerging. He engages in the eternal battle between darkness and light.

Ra is a very benevolent god. He has cared for his human family for thousands of centuries, so he knows all about the emotional struggles, the fears, the disappointments, and the joy of life. Ra will help make your path much easier. There is no need to reinvent the wheel, so ask for his guidance. He will show you the easiest and most efficient way to create what you want. Ra also is a consummate lover, so he can also advise you on matters of the heart.

Atlas

Associated Culture

Greek

Atlas will help you

- Achieve your goals
- Find the inner strength to overcome anything
- Remember to listen to your inner guidance
- Follow directions

Invocation

Ask Atlas to show you the way. Ask him to help you map out your strategies in life. Ask for his assistance and then listen for the quiet whispers. Atlas never fails those who ask for his help.

Atlas was a Titan and one of the firstborn sons of the Earth. He sided with his brothers against Zeus and, as a punishment, was assigned the task of holding up the heavens. He was temporarily relieved of his burden when Hercules asked for his help in retrieving the Golden Apple from the Tree of Life. The apple represented immortality.

Atlas undertook this heroic quest and managed to get the apple. In doing so, he realized how nice it was to be free of his burden. He boldly told Hercules that Hercules would have to continue to hold heaven and earth apart indefinitely. Hercules agreed, but he told Atlas he first needed to get a pillow to cushion his shoulder. Atlas foolishly agreed and took back his burden. Hercules never returned.

Today, an atlas is a book of maps. Atlas shows humans about courage, the power of choice, and the folly of not listening to your inner wisdom. He fought Zeus and wound up carrying the burden of the world. Once free of those burdens, he agreed to take them back even though he knew Hercules would probably never come back. He was able to get the apple off the Tree of Life when everyone else had failed, yet he doomed himself to hold up the heavens for all of eternity. He invites you to learn from his mistakes. What burdens do you needlessly shoulder? Who or what do you resist and in the process set yourself up for pain and suffering?

Ma'at

Associated Culture

Egyptian

Ma'at will help you

- Settle disputes fairly
- Bring order into your home emotionally and physically
- Regulate your menstrual cycle
- Bring honesty into all of your relationships
- See the world in a more expansive manner

Invocation

Ma'at is often shown wearing an ostrich feather or represented by a feather. Ma'at is always willing to help anyone, so simply asking is enough. If you want to have her presence in your life on a regular basis, get a bouquet of ostrich feathers and put them someplace you will see them often.

Ma'at is the goddess of balance, truth, and order. Her name literally means "the truth."

Egyptians believed the universe was an ordered and rational place. It functioned with predictability and regularity. The universe was balanced, both physically and morally. Purity and good deeds were rewarded, and sin was punished. The universe was in perfect balance.

Ma'at was reality, the solid grounding of reality that made the Sun rise, the stars shine, the river flood, and mankind think. The universe and everything in it was sacred in the ancient view of life. "Ethics" was an issue of human will and human permission. It is part of the human world of duality. What is "ethical" for one group is sin for another. But Ma'at invites people to transcend that limited view of ethics. A flower is just a flower; it can't be good or evil, it just is. How can a flower be "false" or "ethical"? It just is. How can the universe be right or wrong? It simply is. That is Ma'at.

She is a winged goddess and the judge of the underworld. A dead person's heart was weighed by Ma'at. If the person had lied or cheated, his heart was eaten by a demon and he died permanently. If he was found to be just, he was allowed to continue to the afterlife. Ma'at was such an influence that being honest and just was referred to as being Ma'at.

Ma'at will help you go beyond the limited vision of a world based on duality. She will help you see your life from the incredibly expansive perspective of recognizing the unity and interconnectedness of everything and everyone.

Yemaya

Associated Culture

African

Yemaya will help you

- Conceive a child
- Have a safe and painless childbirth
- Protect against infidelity
- Create a loving home
- Feel safe and nurtured no matter where you are
- Stay protected from sexual predators

Invocation

One of Yemaya's gifts to humans was the seashell in which her voice could always be heard. Find a large conch shell and hold it to your ear. Listen to the gentle whisper of Yemaya. Ask her for her guidance and protection. She is an incredibly nurturing and powerful ally, so place the shell where you will see it frequently and call upon her when you do.

Yemaya is the ultimate mother goddess. She represents the ebb and flow of life, both the constancy and the endless change of the seasons. Originally a river goddess in Nigeria, she is a nature spirit of home, fertility, love, and family. She brings forth life, is protective, and facilitates change when it is necessary. Yamaya's gentle waves enfold the abundant life forms of the sea.

When the slave traders stole Yemaya's people, she traveled with them in the holds of the slave ships. She comforted them while they suffered on the ships and then helped them adjust to their new homes in faraway lands. She became the goddess of the ocean in order to accompany them.

Yemaya represents a mother's nurturing and love. She is inextricably connected to the affairs of women. Yemaya is the goddess of fertility, children, birthing, and the home. She protects the family. She is the merciful, loving, and nurturing goddess of creation and a deep ocean of comfort for those in need.

African deities are usually depicted with flowing, swirling images of color and joyous movement, representing the elemental energies of nature. Yemaya is associated with azure blue, white, and silver swirls of color. She is also portrayed as a mermaid or a beautiful woman.

Ishtar

Associated Culture

Mesopotamian

Ishtar will help you

- Be an inspiring lover
- Enhance your sexual experiences
- Create a nurturing environment
- Embrace your femininity
- Improve family relations
- Conceive a child

Invocation

Ishtar's symbols are the stars, the moon, the lion, and the dove, so surround yourself with them. She loves the sound of drums, so hold a drum between your legs and play it with complete abandon. Feel the drumbeat moving through your body and ask Ishtar for her help. Allow yourself to feel the warmth of her love and the kindness of her guidance.

Ishtar was the ancient Babylonian goddess of love, fertility, passion, and sexuality. She was honored as the goddess who inspires lovers. She reminds people to stop for a moment and connect with the joyous energy of passion and to remember that she is the one who brings it into your life. At times, Ishtar is shown as a woman holding an urn of life pressed tightly against her stomach.

Sometimes Ishtar is depicted as a heartless woman who kills her lovers. Alternately she is seen as the epitome of the ultimate woman, a compassionate partner, nurturing mother, inspired lover, playful companion, and passionate bed lover. Ishtar is most passionately revered at the time of the full moon, when she invites people to indulge in carefree lovemaking and invites women to celebrate their womanhood. Christians modified Ishtar into the Virgin Mary and incorporated her into their religious practices.

Ishtar is wonderful to call upon if you are feeling underappreciated or judged in any way. If you feel taken advantage of by your partner or your boss, ask Ishtar to come to your aid. She will remind everyone what an incredible being of light you really are.

Cupid

Associated Culture

Roman

Cupid will help you

- Find love
- Heal a broken heart
- Love yourself unconditionally
- Improve all of your relationships

Invocation

The most familiar image of Cupid is seen around Valentine's Day, usually in front of a large red heart. You can use that image to call upon him and write your request on the back of the heart. He loves love, so he will rapidly come to the aid of anyone who asks with an open and loving heart.

Cupid is the Roman god of love and the son of the magnificent goddess Venus. At times he is portrayed as a small, blindfolded, winged boy, carrying a bow and arrow. Whomever he shoots with his arrow is destined to fall in love. Some stories say he was born from a silver or golden egg. Cupid is cute and lovable, but he is also mischievous and dangerous. His arrows contain love, but they also inflict pain.

His wings speak to the spiritual side of love, yet his lofty vantage point often leads to the despair of lost love. He is often a trickster when he chooses to play with human emotions, but ultimately he is the god of love. Cupid reminds humans of the power of love, especially when it is pure and uncontaminated by jealousy, fear, and greedy attachment. From Cupid's perspective, much of what humans call love is really nothing but an attempt to control and manipulate another person. He knows the meaning of true love and knows it means wanting the object of that love to be happy, even if that means the person is meant to love another.

Cupid reminds people that they must first love themselves before they will be able to truly love another. His arrows cause pain only when the hearts they pierce are unsure of their ability to love and care for themselves while having enough room to love and care for another.

Perkūnas

Associated Culture

Lithuanian

Perkūnas will help you

- Prevail in any legal disputes
- Find a fair and just solution to any dispute
- Bring rain during a drought
- Attract abundance
- Have your voice heard

Invocation

Perkūnas is a man of mystery. He loves helping people manifest their deepest dreams. Ask for his help and then let him light the way. If there are any oak trees in your neighborhood, gather a few leaves. You could write your requests on them and let the wind carry them away. When you see an oak tree or watch a magnificent thunderstorm, say hello to Perkūnas and thank him for being in your life.

Perkūnas is the god of lightning, thunder, and storms. He symbolizes the creative forces of courage and success. He is the elemental god of the sky, rain, thunder, and the heavenly fire, lightning. He was the master of the atmosphere, having control over the wind and the water of the sky. He inspires awe with the raw power of a thunderstorm crashing across the countryside. Perkūnas is the god responsible for justice, honesty, and fairness. When enraged by injustice, he directs his wrath at the people causing the harm. His axes always find their mark and contain the symbols of heaven and earth.

Perkūnas is also associated with fertility because without rain the land dries up and all plant life dies. The oak is his sacred tree. Standing beneath the mighty oak, Perkūnas reminds you that anything is possible. Even the smallest acorn contains the possibility of a huge oak tree. If you've had an inkling about something, even the vaguest thought which suggests you might want to change something in your life or create something new, know you can do it. Those gentle stirrings in your heart are often the whispers of the gods reminding you of your divinity and urging you on.

Perkūnas is a mighty god and a powerful ally. His lightning bolts can light up even the darkest night. Ask him to help you, especially when you are unsure about what to do next.

Ancestors

Associated Cultures

Many cultures

The Ancestors will help you

- Heal family issues
- Fill your life with laughter and joy
- Know what you want to create and how to create it
- Live life to the fullest
- Improve all of your relationships

Invocation

Take a few minutes and decide what it is you want to create. If it is your family ancestors you wish to contact, gather some family pictures. If you wish to connect with your spiritual lineage, use an icon or image you are attracted to. Sit quietly with the images and call upon the ancestors. Silently state your request and breathe deeply. Imagine them reaching back through time, lovingly extending their assistance, and know it is so.

The Ancestors are all those who have gone before us. Some traditions have altars specifically designed to honor the Ancestors. There is a thin ribbon stretching back through the mists of time to the moment when your soul first sprung into existence. There are the genealogical ancestors of your physical body, and there are the legions of spiritual guides and ancestors that have helped you throughout the ages. The Ancestors create a matrix of wisdom beyond your comprehension, and they are available to you anytime you ask.

There are many ways to learn, and one of the easiest ways is by tapping into the wisdom of those who have gone before us. Each race has their ancestral heritage, and within it lies the history of their race. There is also the ancestral heritage of the planet, a wisdom that reminds individuals that they are all part of a greater whole. Beyond that lies the wisdom of the godself, which has an unwavering knowledge of the oneness of all beings in the universe.

You can call upon all the Ancestors or specify the ancestors of your family or of your country. They will immediately embrace you with their love, guidance, and wisdom. Use that connection to guide you to a sense of unity, wholeness, and holiness.

Kwan Yin

Associated Cultures

Indian / Asian

Kwan Yin will help you

- Release shame
- Activate compassion and kindness
- Become pregnant
- Connect with your femininity

- Transform your anger
- Experience joy
- Heal physically, mentally, and spiritually
- Embrace being a vegetarian

Invocation

Kwan Yin hears all prayers, so connecting with her is extremely easy. She often stands upon an open lotus flower, so hold a flower and remember to connect with compassion. Once you understand your issue, you could say something like this:

"Kwan Yin, help me to see my life through your loving eyes of compassion.
May all areas of my life be embraced by your wisdom and grace
and be transformed by your love. Guide me now and always."

Kwan Yin is the goddess of compassion and loving-kindness whose name means "One who hears the cries of the world." She holds a willow branch and sprinkles the divine nectar of life on all who come to her. In her other hand, she holds a vase from which she pours the healing waters of life. Kwan Yin is often depicted standing on a dragon, the ancient symbol for spirituality, wisdom, strength, and the power of transformation.

Kwan Yin is the goddess of mercy. Simply by calling upon her with sincerity and an open heart, you can experience rebirth and renewal. She is a truly enlightened being who has vowed to stay upon the Earth until all other beings have achieved enlightenment. She is a virgin goddess who protects women and brings a child to any woman who desires one.

Depictions of Kwan Yin are always graceful, beautiful, and human. She is a goddess who is approachable by all. She radiates a sweet, loving, and gentle femininity that is filled with power and strength. She teaches us to be powerful and create what we want and yet be harmless in a world so filled with violence.

Vishnu

Associated Culture

Hindu

Vishnu will help you

- Create anything you want
- Renew your commitment to yourself and to your spiritual growth
- Sleep soundly and remember your dreams
- Find a lost love

Invocation

Vishnu loves beauty, harmony, and order.
You can write a letter to him or simply ask him for his help.
You might want to light a blue or yellow candle and burn the letter.

Vishnu is considered a major god of Hinduism. He is thought of as the "preserver of the universe," upholding the universal laws. Brahma and Shiva, the two other major Hindu gods, are considered to be the creator and the destroyer of the universe. While Shiva retreats into the forest to meditate, Vishnu immerses himself in the world. He is in constant participation with creation and ensures all is well.

Vishnu sleeps when order prevails in the universe. He floats on the cosmic ocean while the universe unfolds from his dreams. When there is disorder in the universe, Vishnu awakens and either battles with the forces of chaos himself or sends one of his avatars to save the world.

Vishnu has thousands of names. His devotees repeat these names daily as proof of their love and devotion. He is depicted with a blue body, symbolizing the infinite. The garland around his neck is a symbol of the worship he receives as a god; the crown is a symbol of his divine power and supreme authority. His two earrings stand for the dual nature of creation. Vishnu is dressed in yellow, which symbolizes his fight for justice and the destruction of evil. He usually has four arms. He holds a shell, a lotus, a scepter, and a disc. The shell represents Vishnu's relationship with the primordial waters of creation. The lotus is a symbol of spiritual development and cosmic harmony. The scepter is a symbol of power and authority. The disc symbolizes the sun and spiritual illumination.

Vishnu is the god of love and creation. He will show you how to create order in your life and find harmony and balance.

Inti

Associated Culture

Incan

Inti will help you

- Organize your life
- Train an ill-mannered pet
- Remind your son or daughter about respect
- Bring order to any chaotic situation
- Avoid traffic jams

Invocation

Stand facing east early in the morning and call his name. Ask Inti for his guidance and his support. If you find yourself confused during the day, just imagine an image of a bright golden sun and call on him. He loves to bring order to chaos and loving behavior into stressful situations. He is the god of civilized behavior, so ask and he will be there for you.

Inti was the Incan god of the sun. Incans called themselves "Children of the Sun." The sun was worshipped for its ability to bring forth life. Farmers worshipped him, knowing that he could enhance or destroy their crops. Inti taught his children the ways of civilization and then sent them to Earth to teach humans how to live in harmony on this beautiful planet. The Incans believed that silver was made of tears from the moon and gold was created by sweat from the sun.

As well as being the sun god, Inti was the state god and the ancestor of the Incan people. To prove their love for the gods, they built stone structures on the top of the mountains or other sacred locations to honor them. Inti's relationship with the people was harmonious, gentle, and loving. Inti married Pachamama, the great earth goddess, and was one of the most benevolent of the Incan gods.

Inti can help bring joy back into your life. Being the sun god, he can illuminate even the darkest of situations. When you are feeling confused or unsure of what to do next, call upon him.

Blodeuwedd

Associated Culture

Celtic

Blodeuwedd will help you

- Resolve very emotional issues
- Let go of a relationship that no longer serves you
- Speak up for yourself and ask for what you want
- Redirect a wayward child's emotions and behaviors

Invocation

Blodeuwedd is a creature of the night. Her power begins to build at dusk and wanes at dawn. Call upon her when you feel your emotions overriding your intellect. Imagine your spirit taking flight and Blodeuwedd showing you how to create happiness and joy in your life and the lives of others involved. Call upon her every night for a week and watch for a miraculous healing to occur in your life.

Blodeuwedd is the goddess of emotions, representing the powerful forces of desire, destiny, love, and the creative force of spirit. She is aligned with the gentle wisdom of the lunar mysteries and the wisdom of innocence. In the Tarot she is represented by the empress card. Blodeuwedd possesses the power of self-determination to transform life.

Blodeuwedd was created out of the flowers of an oak treec a very powerful tree of love, life, and healing. She was destined to be the bride of Llew, but she fell in love with Goronwy and wanted to be free of Llew. He could only be killed at twilight, wrapped in a fish net, standing with one foot on a cauldron and the other on a goat, and if the weapon had been forged during sacred hours when such work was forbidden. Blodeuwedd asked him to show her how impossible such a position was to achieve by chance. As he demonstrated, Goronwy killed Llew.

He was transformed into an eagle but eventually was restored to human form and killed Goronwy. Blodeuwedd was transformed into an owl, destined to spend eternity haunting the night in loneliness and sorrow, shunned by all other birds.

Blodeuwedd's transformation is symbolic of the mystical relationship between the body, mind, and spirit. The owl imparts the wisdom of objectivity and detachment. Had Blodeuwedd seen her life differently, she could have asked to be released from her vows and pursued her own loves and passions. She reminds women of the importance of being assertive and clearly asking for what they want. She shows people how to use their emotions as a powerful and transformative energy in their lives.

Maeve

Associated Culture

Irish

Maeve will help you

- Create abundance
- Release limiting beliefs
- Find love
- Make better choices
- Organize your life

Invocation

Maeve loves the green hills of Ireland. Light a green candle and call her name. Ask her to help you see how you created what is presently in your life and how to make new choices.

"Maeve, help me to see my life from your limitless perspective so I can release all beliefs that limit my experience of life. Bestow upon me your mystical knowledge so I can embrace all of life. Help me to love with passion and become the sovereign leader in my life."

Maeve was one of the great goddesses of Ireland. She was originally the goddess of the land's sovereignty and its mystic center at Tara. She was able to run faster than horses and wore live birds and animals across her body. Maeve's name means "intoxicating," and her beauty and sexual prowess were. Under the Christian influence, she was demoted to a mortal queen.

Maeve taught the people that the land was sacred and invites them to remember they are the caretakers. The earth isn't something to be owned and abused, but is to be nurtured and loved. As a mortal queen, she was known as the Queen of Ireland. She was a regal woman in charge of her life. She was a queen who got what she wanted when she wanted it.

Maeve's challenge to you is to take total responsibility for your life. She is very clear that being responsible is not associated with being at fault. She explains that being responsible is being accountable for your choices. It is your ability to respond to life rather than react. Maeve challenges you to become the queen of your life and expand your domain. She invites you to become aware of your beliefs and to notice when you are making choices that aren't consistent with what you want to create.

Athena

Athena will help you

- Have success with financial endeavors
- Choose wisely
- Enhance your creativity
- Improve your fashion sense
- Create an elegant home

Invocation

To call upon Athena, light two candles, a red one and a white one. As you light them, ask for her guidance. Invite her into your life and then stand back. She is a power force and will rapidly help you make all the changes that are necessary.

Athena is the goddess of wisdom, arts, industry, justice, and war. Athena and her uncle Poseidon were very fond of several Greek cities. It was decided that whoever brought the finest gift could claim the city as his or her own. Poseidon struck the ground and produced a spring, but it was as salty as the sea. Athena brought the gift of the olive tree, which gave the people shade, oil, food, and wood. The people valued her gift more, so the city became known as Athens. She showed people how to weave the finest fabric and elevated crafts to a heavenly level. As the goddess of war, she showed people how to use discipline and strategy and how to maintain a cool head. She abhorred brutality and encouraged war only to defend hearth and home.

Athena invented the horse bit and that showed humans how to tame horses. She is often associated with the owl, and the most important temple dedicated to her was the Parthenon. She was the first virgin goddess and sprung fully matured from her father's skull wearing her mother's robe and a helmet. Athena is a fierce fighter, but above all else she is the goddess of the city; she is the protector of the family and the finer aspects of civilization. She is considered the embodiment of wisdom, reason, and purity.

Athena is the all-knowing goddess, and her counsel, though often brief, is profound and transformative. She is an elegant goddess to call upon and will show you how to bring beauty and joy into your life. Even though she is the goddess of war, her gift of the olive tree shows that she knows a great deal about peace, too.

Great Spirit

Associated Culture

Native American

The Great Spirit will help you

- Heal your mind, body, and spirit
- Release stress
- Improve the environment
- Create a loving home
- Make your garden grow
- Plan your future

Invocation

The Great Spirit is always there and available, so calling upon him is a matter of expanding your awareness. Open your heart and your mind to his presence. Practice seeing the spirit in everything. Take the time to bless your food before you eat, give thanks for your car before you drive anywhere, and thank your home before you enter it for protecting you from the elements. Explain your cares and concerns to the Great Spirit and know he will guide you and direct you.

In Native American culture the Great Spirit is the creator. He is a personal spiritual being; he is in everything and everyone. He is part of the very fabric of life. The Great Spirit shows the people how to live, what seed to plant, and how to harvest, and he reminds the people of the sacred nature of everything. Before an animal is killed or a plant is harvested, a prayer of thanks is given. The Great Spirit is closer to the Hindu concept of gods than the Christian idea.

It is the Great Spirit that gives life to everything. He is present in the trees, the sky, and the grass. He is in the food you eat and the water you drink. When you begin to connect with the Great Spirit, life takes on a new depth and every act becomes sacred. If you allow yourself to really feel the presence of the Great Spirit in everything, the colors become more vibrant and the wind becomes a wonderful guide and companion. You begin to see and feel things previously unavailable to you.

The Great Spirit is a wonderful entity to get to know. He will affect all areas of your life in a positive and loving manner. As human beings, we tend to be a bit arrogant and forget that everything in the world is alive and has consciousness even if it is different from ours. When you feel the presence of consciousness in everything, you realize that you are part of the whole and can no longer abuse the planet that is your mother.

Sarasvati

Associated Culture

Hindu

Sarasvati will help you

- Write music, poetry, or even a term paper
- Access ancient wisdoms
- Quiet your mind
- Conceive a child
- Enhance your creativity
- Do well on exams

Invocation

Sarasvati is an elegant goddess. She loves beautiful things and soothing music. Before you ask for her help, create a soothing and inviting environment, either internally or externally. Once you feel ready, call her name softly three times, wait a few moments, and then call her name again, a little bit louder. You will feel her respond. Simply remain open to her love and guidance.

Sarasvati is the Hindu goddess of all arts: music, painting, sculpture, dance, and writing. She gave humans the gift of writing so her songs could be written down and preserved. Sarasvati is often shown riding on the back of a swan or peacock. She has her four arms, with which she plays the lute or the drum and bestows jeweled blessings. She is an elegant goddess whose words pour from her like a sweetly flowing river. She is a jealous rival of the goddess of wealth, Lakshmi. If you are pursuing only wealth, be assured that Sarasvati's gifts will desert you.

Sarasvati is also considered the goddess of learning, intelligence, crafts, arts, and skills. She is considered knowledge itself. Thus many students worship her for her blessings. She is often depicted with a white complexion and is quite beautiful and graceful. She sits on a lotus, which symbolizes that she is founded upon knowledge of the Absolute truth. She has the ability to show you how to have a direct experience of that Truth.

In one of her right hands, Sarasvati holds prayer beads. In her left hand, she holds a book of secular knowledge. Her four arms represent her unlimited power in the four directions. She also represents creativity and combines power and intelligence, which is the basis of true creativity. Sarasvati is also considered the mother of the universe and is connected with fertility.

Hestia

Hestia will help you

- Resolve matters of the home
- Solve legal issues
- Conduct any type of ceremony
- Deepen your connection with the spiritual realms

Invocation

Traditionally, Hestia was offered small gifts of food. You could prepare a food basket before you ask for her assistance and then perhaps donate it to a homeless shelter. Spend a few minutes composing your thoughts and then simply say, "Hestia, please help me with [then explain your problem]."

Hestia is the goddess of the hearth. She originated the concept of family and is the founder of the concept of the state. She maintains public reverence for the gods. Her parents are Cronos and Rhea, and she is the sister of Zeus, Poseidon, Hades, Hera, and Demeter. She is one of the twelve Olympians. Hestia was invoked at the opening and closing of all public ceremonies in ancient Greece. Her sacred fire was kept burning in the center of the city to remind people of her presence and the importance of home and country. Those wanting protection from the government would go to her sacrificial fire and ask for her help. In the temple of Delphi, her sacred fire was the center of Greek religious life.

Hestia is a gentle presence and is often shown in artwork with a serious expression that reminds the viewer of the solemn nature of her task in life. She will help you connect with the power, wonder, and magic of the mystical realms of the divine universe. Hestia is wonderful to call upon before you ask any other angels, saints, or deities to help you. If you can find a small statue of her, place it somewhere in your home to assure a harmonious family life. If you have an interest in politics, she will help you elect the candidate of your choice, one who would truly be of service to the people. She will also help oust uncaring or corrupt public officials.

Odin

Odin will help you

- Write poetry or a term paper
- Improve your musical abilities
- Speak to a loved one who has died
- Access your inner wisdom

Invocation

Light a yellow candle before you ask for Odin's guidance. Because he has mastered the runes, you might want to purchase a set of them. Runes are a wonderful tool for accessing your inner wisdom, and Odin will gladly show you how to use them.

Odin is the Norse god of war and death. He is also the god of poetry, magic, prophecy, and wisdom. He lives in Valhalla, where the fallen warriors are taken. Odin has only one eye and it shines like the sun. He traded his other eye for a drink from the Well of Wisdom, from which he gained an immense amount of wisdom. In one of his many adventures, he was able to obtain a profound understanding of the ancient runes. He is able to see into the future and can help you use that knowledge to avoid any pitfalls. Odin is a master at using whatever resources are at hand to create a wonderful outcome for everyone involved.

Odin hung on the world tree for nine days, pierced by his own spear. He learned nine powerful songs, and the meaning of the eighteen runes. He gained a tremendous amount of knowledge and wisdom, which he is more than willing to share with anyone who asks. Odin has the ability to speak to the dead and can question the wisest among them.

Odin will show you how to settle family battles, give you the wisdom to talk with your teenager, and help you to get a troublesome mate to hear you when you explain your wants and needs. He can charm your boss or sweet-talk your lover. With his gift of prophecy and infinite wisdom, your ability to make wise choices will be greatly enhanced.

Ancient Ones

Associated Cultures

Many cultures

Ancient Ones will help you

- Experience happiness no matter what is happening
- Connect with your divinity

- Invite abundance into all areas of your life
- Embrace life and live passionately
- Savor every moment

Invocation

Light a candle, stand out under the moonlight, or build a bonfire. Take a few moments to connect with the light and then ask the Ancient Ones for their assistance. Open your heart and your mind to them. You may feel a gentle wind embrace you or simply feel loved and connected. Just ask for them and they will be there.

Many spiritual traditions talk about the Ancient Ones. The stories about them vary, but the common theme is that they have a vast amount of knowledge, incredible wisdom, wonderful compassion, and a deep love for humanity. In some traditions, they are believed to be from a different universe, while in others, they are considered deities. Regardless of the explanation, they are a powerful presence and exert a huge influence on this planet.

When you are willing to allow the Ancient Ones into your life, your perspective on life changes immediately. They view life as an incredible gift and will help you to see the perfection in everything. If you look back at

something you felt was very traumatic five years ago, chances are that today it has a minimal effect on your life. The Ancient Ones will help you realize you don't have to wait five years. You can change your perspective right now and skip the necessity of waiting to feel better tomorrow.

The Ancient Ones' main desire is to remind human beings to awaken in the moment. They realize how precious each moment is and try to help people savor every minute of life. They see life from a grander perspective and will invite you to do the same. The Ancient Ones absolutely know that everything is perfect and will help you to see that perfection as well.

La'amaomao

Associated Culture

Hawaiian

La'amaomao will help you

- Shake loose anything that no longer serves you
- Move into a new home
- Change jobs
- Find a new love

Invocation

Go outside and feel the wind. Your words contain the power of creation in each syllable and phrase. Take a deep breath and call, "La'amaomao." Then launch your request into the wind. Let the wind carry your words into the cosmos and know they will come back to you manifested in physical reality.

If you have an issue you can't seem to release, stand in the wind. Imagine La'amaomao moving through you. Don't resist; just imagine the wind passing through your body, cleansing you of anything that no longer serves you.

La'amaomao is the goddess of the winds of Hawaii and lives on the powerful island of Molokai. One literal translation of her name is "distant sacredness." The Hawaiians were voyagers, so the winds were very important in their lives. The different types of winds brought the weather. Each wind has a different name, and it is said that if you know its name and know how to call it, you can command it.

You cannot see the invisible wind until it touches something; only then can you see its path as it moves over the land. You can hear the wind as it goes by and feel it caress your face or rustle your clothing. It can cool you off on a warm day or chill you to the bone. La'amaomao reminds you that your days on this planet are numbered. She suggests you savor each and every moment. La'amaomao can reach into the very heart of your being, touch your soul, and remind you of who and what you are.

Next time you go outside, notice the wind. Call La'amaomao and feel her gentle response. Spend time observing the winds. Watch as the wind lifts a leaf or a piece of paper. The wind is a very powerful force on this planet, and so is La'amaomao. Hawaiians respect nature and know they are part of this magnificent energy system called the universe. Ask La'amaomao to help you find your place in the cosmos. Ask her to help you feel connected, part of the wonder and magic called life.

Thoth

Associated Culture

Egyptian

Thoth will help you

- Find enlightened compromises
- Write and enhance your creativity
- Hear your intuition
- Connect with your divine wisdom
- Attract magic and miracles

Invocation

When you want some of Thoth's wisdom and magic, go outside and
stand in the light of the moon. Raise your hands over your head.
With an open heart and mind, call his name and invite him into your life.

Thoth is the god of wisdom, the inventor of writing, a patron of scribes, and the divine mediator. He is a lunar deity usually depicted with a crescent moon on his head. He values wisdom and is the keeper of the divine wisdoms. As with most Egyptian deities, there are many different stories regarding his parentage. In some, he is the son of Ra, while in another story, he springs from the head of Seth.

Thoth's wisdom was sought by many of the gods. He was often present for the judgment of the dead. He was also the messenger of the gods. He is a very powerful god committed to love, gratitude, the wonders of divinity, and the magical properties of the universe.

Thoth's magical abilities were thought to be so great the Egyptians believed he wrote the mythical "Book of Thoth." If a person read this sacred book, he or she would become the most powerful magician in the world. The book was written by Thoth with his own hand. It was a dangerous and deadly book. If the reader failed to comprehend the wisdoms it contained, the book would bring nothing but pain and tragedy. But if the reader really understood the secrets of the gods—these secrets said to be hidden in the stars—their lives would become magical and filled with miracles.

Thoth's secret message is one of love and gratitude. He knows life is a sacred and divine gift. There are no tests or trials, just opportunities for a person to either deepen their connection with their spirit or with their limited small selves.

Great Mother

Associated Culture

Many cultures

The Great Mother will help you

- Silence your restless mind
- Embrace your spirit
- Have a harmonious family

- Connect with your inner wisdom
- Improve your intuition
- Fill your life with synchronicity

Invocation

"Great Mother, I invite you into my life. I welcome your love, wisdom, and guidance. Please show me the way of joy and wisdom. Bring your laughter into my life so I may find my happiness and fill my life with your love. I give thanks for all the gifts you have bestowed upon me and open my heart and my mind to you. May my path be broad and my way be made easy."

The Great Mother has many names and is part of many traditions. For some people, she is thought of as the Earth mother, while for others, she is great goddess of creation. She represents the feminine principle, the womb of creation, and the love and wisdom of all time. She is the energy that invites you to go within to connect with the silence that lives deep in your sacred space. She guides people toward a deepening connection with the essence of who and what they really are.

The Great Mother regulates the flow of life, the cycle of birth and death, and the ebb and flow of the seasons. She has the ability to control the weather and can easily influence human emotions; she can bring joy into even the most stressful situation.

When you are starting a new endeavor or want to make substantial changes in your life, call upon her. If your relationship seems a bit strained or you would like to conceive a child, ask for her assistance. If your child is being rebellious or exhibiting self-destructive behaviors, she will help you improve your communication so you can create a more loving and supportive relationship. If you want to break free from an addiction, she will help you set yourself free. Freedom, joy, abundance, love, and laughter are her hallmarks.

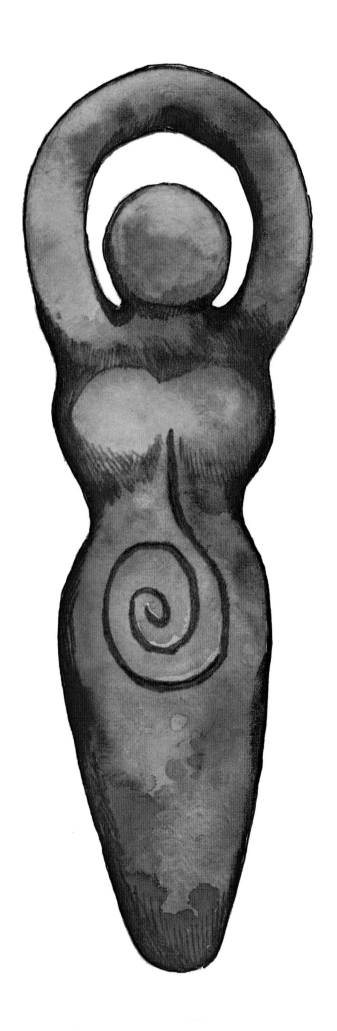

Sybil

Associated Culture

Greek

Sybil will help you

- Talk to a loved one who has died
- See into the future so you can more easily make decisions
- Connect with your own inner wisdom
- Realize what a wonderful and valuable person you are

Invocation

You don't need to sit in a cave to connect with Sybil's wisdom. Just sit quietly and ask her to speak to you. You will often "hear" her answer while you write in your journal. She gladly shares her insights with anyone who asks and is willing to take the time to listen. Make sure you wait for her reply.

In the ancient world, there were ten famous female prophets, one each from Persia, Libya, Delphi, Samos, Cimmeria, Erythraea, Tibur, Marpessus, and Phrygia. The most famous, Sybil, was from Cumae, near Naples. Sybil lived in a cave, which was rediscovered in 1932. It had a 60-foot-high ceiling and a 375-foot entrance passageway.

Sybil wrote her prophecies on leaves. Which she placed at the mouth of her cave. If no one came to collect them, they were scattered by winds and never read. The leaves were sometimes bound into books. Legend says Sybil once brought nine volumes of her prophecies to Tarquin II of Rome, offering to sell them to him at an outrageous price. He refused, so she burned three volumes, offering the remaining six for the same high price. Again he refused. She burned three more volumes and again asked the original price. This time the king's curi-osity was so great he purchased the remaining three Sibylline prophecies. These volumes were carefully kept in the Capitol and consulted only on momentous occasions by the Senate.

In one myth, Sybil of Cumae gained her powers through attracting the attention of the sun god, Apollo. He offered her anything she wanted if she would spend a single night with him. She asked for as many years of life as the grains of sand she could hold in her hand. He granted her wish, but she still refused to sleep with him. He cursed her with eternal life but refused to give her eternal youth. Sybil's name means "cave dweller." Her oracular spirit spoke through a succession of priestesses in the sacred cave of Cumae, which was famed as an entrance to the underworld. Sybil's priestesses were able to call upon the dead for necromantic interviews.

Wandjina

Associated Culture

Australian

The Wandjina will help you

- Create harmony and ease
- Make new friends
- Get established in a new area
- Find a new home

Invocation

The Wandjina are closely aligned with nature and magnificent rock formations. Decide what you would like to ask them to help you with and then light an orange candle. Step outside and watch the sunset and know that they are working behind the scenes.

The Wandjina control the seasons and bring the rains. In a dry land, water is equivalent to life, so the Wandjina are the creation gods. The Wandjina have a deep and meaningful relationship with the heritage and culture of the Aboriginal people. The Wandjina are ancestral beings who rose up out of the oceans. They created the landscape and then were absorbed into the rock formations. The Wandjina are still depicted in contemporary Aboriginal paintings. For centuries, images were found on bark *coolamons*, or baskets used for food gathering, on cradles for newborns, and on ceremonial boomerangs and shields. The Wandjina are part of the lives of the tribes who have for many years lived and survived in the country where Wandjina carvings are found.

The Wandjina command respect and have great powers. When you please them, you thrive, and when you insult them, they bring their great wrath to bear. Legends say that they once were so disheartened by the behavior of humans that they opened their mouths and released a torrent of water. They caused a great flood that devastated the landscape and wiped out the human race.

After the flood, the Wandjina spread out to different parts of the land. They created a new society and helped humans to multiply. They stopped opening their mouths and eventually they went away. When the Wandjina are shown in human form, they have round faces, painted in white, with eyes and noses but no mouths.

The Wandjina are powerful beings of creation and will help bring abundance and joy to your life. If you call upon them, they will sprinkle magic and miracles on your world.

Artemis/Diana

Associated Cultures

Greek / Roman

Artemis/Diana will help you

- Heal the pain of sexual abuse
- Conceive a child
- Give birth with joy and ease
- Avoid heartbreak
- Choose a loving partner

Invocation

Imagine Artemis sitting beside you and talk to her as you would your best friend. Tell her about all your hopes, your dreams, and desires. Share your heartbreaks and your failures with her. Allow her love to reach deep into your being and heal your deepest wounds. She is the Great Mother and is capable of incredible miracles, so ask for her help and know it is always given.

Artemis is the sister of Apollo. She was born several days before him so she could help her mother with his delivery. She is a virgin but is considered the goddess of fertility and easy births. Artemis is considered the original mother without a spouse because all humans are her children. She takes her chastity seriously and adamantly defends a woman's right to choose her partners. Her wrath is nothing to fool with and admonishes no one to try to shame the Mother. She was also considered the goddess of nature and was portrayed as a huntress accompanied by a deer. Diana is Latin for "goddess," and she was the Roman equivalent of Artemis.

Her temple was the last of the Great Goddess Temples and was active well into the Christian era. It was at the temple dedicated to Artemis and Diana in Ephesus that the Christian Church declared Mary to be the "mother of God" in 413 C.E., and she was given many of the goddess titles, including "Mother of All" and "Queen of Heaven." Some believe this was an attempt to legitimize the Christian religion and replace the beloved goddess with Mary.

Artemis was always a friend to mortals. She was often seen dancing through the countryside in silver sandals, bestowing her divine protection to wild beasts and the very young. Her temples were always colorful and inviting.

Morgan la Fay

Associated Culture

Celtic

Morgan la Fay will help you

- Attract a new lover
- Find a new job
- Locate a new place to live
- Heal a sick child
- Unearth your hidden desires

Invocation

Morgan la Fay is an elegant woman who likes the finer things in life. Drape yourself in a beautiful piece of white linen or a piece of golden cloth and light a purple candle. Then simply and concisely state your purpose. You may feel a stirring in your heart, see the candle begin to flicker, or see the curtains move even though the windows are closed.

Morgan la Fay is known as an evil enchantress, a fairy, and a goddess. In some versions of her story, she is the half-sister of King Arthur and tricks him into conceiving a son with her. As a goddess, she is a shape-shifter with great wisdom and incredible powers of healing. She has the ability to manifest magical birds and is transported from her home in a dragon boat. She is the goddess of the sea and the underworld. In some legends, she is the Lady of the Lake. As the goddess of the underworld, she transported Arthur's body. She is protecting his body until his regeneration is complete and it is time for him to rise again.

Morgan la Fay is an immortal being who is a great artist and a healer. She is the divinity of battle. There is a dispute as to whether her surname means "fairy" or "fate." Morgan la Fay will show you how to make changes rapidly in your life. She is able to see into the future, so she can show you the shortest way to manifest your dreams. As the goddess of the ocean, she has sway over all living beings because water is the major component in all living entities.

In most stories, she was very devious and manipulative, but she accomplished whatever she wanted. If you really want to manifest something and aren't particularly worried about how you accomplish it, she's your woman.

Fates

Associated Culture

Greek

The Fates will help you

- Connect with a larger sense of self
- See the rhythms of life more clearly
- Embrace magic
- Overcome grief
- Love more fully

Invocation

You could say, "Fates, I call upon your merciful presence. Please help guide and direct me. Help me savor each moment and make choices based on love instead of fear. Help me to see [explain your dilemma] from your lofty perspective. I give thanks for your presence in my life and for your wisdom and grace."

The Fates are the goddesses who control the destiny of everyone from birth until death. Clotho is the spinner who spins the thread of a person's life. Lachesis decides how much time each person is allowed. Atropos is the Fate who cuts the thread of life, thus deciding when you die. Even the other gods are subject to the whims of the Fates. The priests and priestesses of the Fates are always oracles or soothsayers.

The Fates were often depicted as ugly old hags, cold-hearted and merciless. They laugh at people and the gods' feeble attempts at cheating fate because the Fates always prevail. They are neither heartless nor merciless. They are part of the natural rhythm of life. Life and death are part of the earth experience. Without death, there would be very little incentive to fully savor life. Humans aren't victimized by the Fates, although that is often how the adventure is portrayed. The Fates give humans a framework in which to experience life.

The Fates remind us that there is a season for everything and there is a natural order to the universe. They are loving, compassionate beings whose only wish for human beings is for them to fully enjoy their time on Earth. They remind each person to savor this moment because it is the only time they will ever have to experience it.

Poli'ahu

Associated Culture

Hawaiian

Poli'ahu will help you

- Defuse even the most volatile situations
- Transform your relationships
- Create abundance
- Connect with your deepest wisdom
- See beyond the mists of illusion

Invocation

Even though Poli'ahu is the goddess of snow, she has a warm heart and
generous nature. Call her name several times and ask for her assistance.
Light a silvery white candle and allow it to illuminate your life.
Her aid will come to you in many wonderful ways. Just remain open
to the unusual and know her guidance will come to you.

One day it is said the snow goddess Poli'ahu and her friends came down from Mauna Kea to the grassy slopes of Hamakua for holua sledding. Pele loved he'eholua, the exhilarating race that took place on sleds with runners set only six inches apart. A racer would hold the holua sled in her right hand, grab hold of the left side of the sled, and then plummet downwards toward the ocean.

Pele appeared in the guise of a beautiful young woman, and the unsuspecting Poli'ahu welcomed her to join in their sport. As the ground grew hotter and hotter, Poli'ahu realized the beautiful stranger was none other than Pele, her archrival. Pele sent fire fountains after Poli'ahu as she fled to the summit. Red hot lava licked at the edges of Poli'ahu's white mantle, but she grasped her robe and managed to escape.

Poli'ahu, unleashed snow from the frozen clouds overhead. Pele sent rivers of lava down the hillside, which cooled and hardened into stone. From time to time, Pele continues to hurl fire and lava from Mauna Loa and Kilauea, but legend says that Poli'ahu always gains the upper hand in these battles. Her melting snow creates streams and rivers that feed the fertile valleys and give the Hamakua Coast and North Kohala a green, misty surrealistic beauty.

Sedna

Associated Culture

Inuit

Sedna will help you

- Know what will make your lover happy
- Stay warm
- Connect with abundance

- Find anything, even the perfect outfit
- Throw a wonderful party

Invocation

Sedna is a warm and caring goddess. She will surely answer you if you ask
sincerely. If you aren't sure you are willing to make the necessary changes, ask
her to help you find this willingness. She knows about dashed hopes and dreams,
so she will do everything in her power to help you avoid disappointment.

Sedna is the sea goddess and a master of animals, especially the mammals of the sea, such as the seals, whales, and dolphins. Her father is Anguta, the creator-god. In one tale, she was a beautiful young woman and a virgin who was lured into marriage by an evil bird spirit. When her father tried to rescue her, the spirit caused such a huge storm that it threatened the existence of the people. In desperation, her father threw her into the angry sea. There are many different versions, but in all of them Sedna's father sends her to her death. But in all the tales she descends into the depths of the ocean and becomes the Goddess of Sea Creatures. As such, she

became a vital deity, eagerly worshipped by hunters who depended on her goodwill to supply food.

Sedna will help you connect with the core of your being, but she will ask you some questions. What are you fooling yourself about? Do you say you want to get in shape and then consistently overeat and put off going to the gym? Is your checkbook balanced and do you pay off your credit cards each month, or does your debt continue to grow? Can you look at yourself in the mirror and love who you see? What gifts do you stop yourself from receiving? Are you willing to make any changes necessary to allow an abundance of bounty into your life now?

Aphrodite

Associated Culture

Greek

Aphrodite will help you

- Unleash your passion
- Enhance your sexuality
- Learn to love with all your heart
- Discover how to savor every moment

Invocation

Aphrodite is very easy to work with and is always available to help bring more love into the world. Put on your favorite music, light a candle, and call her name. You could say a simple prayer like this: "Aphrodite, goddess of love, please open my heart to your guidance and direction. Help me to see the world through your eyes and learn to respond with your graciousness and passion."

In Greek mythology, Aphrodite was the goddess of love, beauty, and sexual rapture. She was born when Uranus, the father of the gods, was castrated and had his genitals thrown into the ocean. The sea began to churn and Aphrodite arose out of the ocean. Zeus married her to Hephaestus, who was the blacksmith of the gods. He made her a finely crafted gold girdle and wove magic into the ornaments. Unfortunately, it made her even more irresistible than she already was. Aphrodite loved and was loved by many gods and mortals.

Aphrodite will teach you about love, lust, and the primal, life-giving energy of sex. She will also teach you about tenderness, loyalty, and the difference between unconditional and conditional love. She will show you that loving yourself is one of the greatest gifts and that until you love yourself, you can't really love anyone else.

She reminds you what a gift a body is and how magnificent sensuality can be. Whether you are eating a strawberry or having passionate sex, she will show you how to fully savor the experience. As the goddess of love, she will show you how to use your five senses to the fullest. She will show you how to use your body to enjoy life in ways you never thought possible.

Lilinoe

Associated Culture

Hawaiian

Lilinoe will help you

- Remain on your true path
- Connect with your life's purpose
- Avoid obstacles
- Invite ease and joy into your life

Invocation

Take a deep breath and allow your request to ring forth.
Speak her name with a loving and lyrical voice. Go out early in
the morning when the mists are still rising or turn on the shower
and fill the room with steam. She will instantly respond to you.

Lilinoe is one of four maiden goddesses with white mantles, associated with the snow-covered mountains of Mauna Kea and Mauna Loa. The goddesses are known to be both very beautiful and extremely intelligent. They were all bitter enemies of the goddess Pele and represent the eternal struggle between fire and water, heat and cold. Because the runoff from the mountains provides fresh water to the lower lands, these goddesses of the mountain are highly regarded.

Mauna Kea has long been a sacred place to the Hawaiian people. The mountain is revered as the embodiment of the *piko*, or umbilical cord, which connects Hawaiians back through time to their ancestral origin as descendants of the gods. It is the home of *Poli'ahu*, the goddess of snow, and her sister *Lilinoe*, the goddess of mist.

Lilinoe's mists can blind you to the path or open to show you the way. As the mists of the mountain, she moves with a great majesty. When she blocks the sun and obliterates the way, you will find yourself chilled to the bone. She is inviting you to reconnect with the warmth of your spirit. She is a loving and kind goddess and impedes your progress only when she knows the path you are on will bring you heartache. Lilinoe will guide you unerringly to your happiness and highest purpose.

She will show you the way and assist you in creating a profound connection to your innate divinity and wisdom. Ask for her help and watch the mists of confusion lift. She will remind you that confusion and hardship signal you are going the wrong way. When you are in alignment with your spirit, she will reward you with tenderness and ease.

Vulcan

Associated Culture

Roman

Vulcan will help you

- Overcome fear
- Try new things
- Forge an incredibly exciting career
- Light the sexual fire in a relationship
- Create whatever you want when you want it

Invocation

Vulcan is the god of fire, so sitting beside a roaring fire will definitely get his attention. You could also light a bunch of candles and state your request clearly and concisely.

Vulcan is the god of fire, especially destructive fire, and of craftsmanship. His forge is beneath Mount Etna. It is there that Vulcan, along with his helpers, forges weapons for the gods and the heroes. Vulcan's temples were usually located outside the cities because of the dangerous nature of fire.

The word *volcano* comes from the small island of Vulcano, situated in the Mediterranean Sea near Sicily. People living in Vulcano believed it was the chimney for Vulcan's forge. They thought the hot lava fragments and clouds of dust erupting from Vulcano came from his forge as he created thunderbolts for Jupiter, the king of the gods, and weapons for Mars, the god of war.

Vulcan can show you how to create joy out of hardship and love out of sadness. He is an incredible craftsman. As the blacksmith of the gods, he can show you how to create anything. You can forge new territory by exploring new concepts; you can travel the world, both inner and outer; and you can experiment with new ways of acting and being. You can ask him for the courage to be outrageously happy and incredibly successful.

Kali

Associated Culture

Hindu

Kali will help you

- Release your fears
- Achieve orgasms and have incredible sex
- Create more time
- Connect with your divinity

- Overcome your limitations
- Move beyond prejudice
- Manifest your dreams

Invocation

Devotees often draped her statues with flowers, so when you wish to call upon her, liberally sprinkle flowers around. If you'd like to vastly increase your enjoyment before a sexual encounter, sprinkle your bed with rose water and ask for her assistance. Because she is the consummate mother, a simple request, such as "Kali, help me," is all that is needed.

Kali is the Hindu mother goddess. Her name comes from a Sanskrit word that can be translated as "time" or "black." She is the symbol of destruction and destroys ignorance while blessing those who seek knowledge of God, Goddess, and all there is. Her appearance is often fearsome. As the consort of Shiva, she is often seen dancing with him or in sexual union. The supreme mistress of the universe, Kali is often associated with the five elements, and is the keeper of time. She is also the goddess of salvation and is able to help us release fear.

Kali has four arms and hands. The left hands usually hold the sword and a severed head. The sword represents divine knowledge, and the human head signifies the limitations of Ego. Her right hands are held in blessing, which signifies her willingness to guide people and help them overcome their limitations. She is often portrayed as being very dark, which represents the un-manifest aspects of reality. Out of the void, out of the darkness comes everything. Kali transcends all form, existed before time began, and will continue to exist long after time ceases.

Kali is usually nude. Her nudity represents total illumination, and she is often described as being garbed by the sky. Kali is a bright fire of truth that cannot be hidden by ignorance. She shows us how to live life beyond the illusionary effects of maya (deceptive beliefs).

Kali is considered the kindest and most loving of all the Hindu goddesses, and she is seen as the great protector. She teaches us about the dynamic and creative nature of pure consciousness. Kali will teach you how to transcend everything yet exclude nothing. She is the epitome of pure, unconditional love.

Sphinx

Associated Culture

Egyptian

The Sphinx will help you

- Release your issues at a core level
- Connect with your inspiration
- Access ancient, divine wisdom
- Become the creator of your life

Invocation

The Sphinx is a powerful mythical force. As soon as you call upon her, she will smile broadly and celebrate your readiness to seek her. Imagine yourself standing in front of the Sphinx and asking for her help. Expect to have more questions than answers at first, and know your freedom lies on the other side of the answers.

The Sphinx appears in Greek mythology as a creature with a woman's head and breasts, a dog's body, a lion's paws, an eagle's wings, and the tail of the serpent who questioned Oedipus. To the ancient Egyptians, the Sphinx symbolized the Nile with its seasons of rebirth. She was also a manifestation of the goddess of birth and of death. The Sphinx in Egypt was built as a guardian of the horizons and of the rising and setting sun. She held the keys to the doors of wisdom.

On their journey to deep knowing and wisdom, the initiates had to confront the challenges that the Sphinx posed. In Greek mythology, she guarded the doorway through which an initiate must pass before accessing the divine mysteries. She sat on a high rock and asked all who wanted to pass the following riddle: "What animal is that which in the morning goes on four feet, at noon on two, and in the evening upon three?" She killed those who could not solve the riddle and tell her it was a human being.

The Sphinx won't let you pass until you respond to her challenge. She asks you: How can you meet the challenges in your life and transform all the aspects of your being? Where in your psyche do you fear to explore? What issues have you been running from? What issues do you blame the people, places, and things in your life for? Would you prefer to change jobs or relationships rather than look at the real cause of your dissatisfaction? What do you need to release, and what do you need to embrace?

The Grandfather

Associated Culture

Native American

The Grandfather will help you

- Let go of the past
- Connect with your soul
- Invite passion into your life
- Tap into your creative abilities to manifest your desires

Invocation

The Grandfather sits in the center of your reality waiting for your call. He sits in a large stone circle surrounded by nature or at the edge of the sea. Imagine going over to him and seeing the love in his eyes when he greets you. He reaches out and holds your hands and asks you how he can help you. Explain your request and then wait patiently for his reply. His magic is profound and very powerful. He may speak to you or send you signs as you move through your day. You can know in your heart of hearts that he is there for you and he will help you.

The Grandfather is an ancient part of many myths of creation. He is an ancient man filled with incredible wisdom. He gently stands at the edge of your reality waiting for you to call upon him. As soon as you ask him, he will reach out with his heart and his mind to help you in any way possible.

He has a weather-beaten, deeply wrinkled face. His hands are spindly and gnarled. The Grandfather's eyes are like pools of deep water, and when he looks at you, his eyes seem to look into the depths of your soul. If you look closely into your eyes, you can see the light of your soul reflected.

Grandfather will help you see beyond your limited perspective into the realm of the great mystery. He was born before the mists of time and will exist long after time ceases to exist. He is a powerful creative force and loves helping people create magic and miracles in their lives.

Manannán

Associated Culture

Celtic

Manannán will help you

- Let go of any old emotional baggage
- Connect with the magic of the moment
- Find a wonderful partner
- Speak to a loved one who has died

Invocation

Stand near some moving water and call his name. You could stand by the sea, a stream, a fountain, or in the shower. Allow yourself to connect with his generous spirit and loving nature. He will be an immense support for you when everything seems to be going wrong.

Manannán is the god of the mist and as mysterious as it as well. He is the son of the deity Lir. Father and son are both gods of the sea. He lives on an island called Emain Ablach, where mystical trees bare a mystical fruit that imparts immortality when eaten. His island is part of the Land of Promise. As the god of the sea, he protects the land as well as the gates between this world and the Otherworld.

Manannán is a strong warrior, very noble and handsome. He has many skills and talents, including many magical powers. He has the ability to control illusions. He wears a great cloak that catches the light and radiates rich colors like the sea. Manannán has a magic bag made from the flesh of a crane which contains all the mysteries of the universe. He is very generous with his gifts and has bestowed many other gods with his magical powers. He is the father of Aine, goddess of love and fertility.

As keeper of the gates between the two worlds, he symbolizes the vast expanse of the collective consciousness that enfolds the tiny island of our conscious mind. He is the guardian between our various states of consciousness, and he can help you awaken to the truth of who and what you are. Manannán invites you to travel between the worlds to a place of peace, joy, confidence, and inner courage. He is a wonderful guide and will help you use your truly magical nature.

Inanna

Associated Culture

Sumerian

Inanna will help you

- Find creative solutions to difficult problems
- Find a soul mate
- Create abundance
- Heal problematic relationships

Invocation

When you call Inanna, you will often feel a gentle breeze begin to stir or a loving caress on your right cheek. She is powerful presence and an incredible helpmate. Write a letter asking for her help. Tell her clearly what the problem is and ask her to help rectify it. Ask her to use her wisdom and love to help you find the solution rather than telling her exactly what you would like to see happen. Her perspective is far more expansive than yours. Then draw eight-sided stars on it and know her help is on the way. You can burn the letter or bury it in the woods.

Inanna is the goddess of love, fertility, and war. She is the queen of life and light. Inanna is considered the daughter of both the sun god and the god of the moon. Her name means "queen of the sky." She is often depicted as a richly dressed goddess or at times as a naked woman. Her symbol is an eight-pointed star.

Inanna is responsible for the seasons. She journeyed into the underworld to face her sister Ereshkigal, who ruled the realm of the dead. When her sister sentenced her to death, all the plants died and nothing could grow on the earth anymore. The god Enki intervened, and it was decided she could live again if someone took her place. She sent her unfaithful husband to replace her, and it was decided he would rule the underworld for half of the year.

Inanna's journey and return home can be seen as the inner journey you take in order to transform your life. Symbolically, it can be seen as the meditative journey into the silence of your mind from which you return with great spiritual insights and a renewed zest for life. She will help you find that still place within yourself so you can connect with your innate inner wisdom and the place where you know only joy. Inanna will help you find and follow your bliss.

Valkyries

Associated Culture

Norse

Valkyries will help you

- Overcome all of life challenges
- Love fully and completely
- Find the perfect mate
- Have the courage to launch a new career
- Connect with your divine nature

Invocation

Light a tall white candle and ask the Valkyries to guide and direct you.
They are the essence of bravery, loyalty, and strength. Open your heart
to them and feel their strength and courage fill your entire being.

The Valkyries are also called the "choosers of the slain." Beautiful young women, they rode winged horses and were armed with helmets and spears. When Odin needed brave warriors for an upcoming battle, the Valkyries scouted battlefields to choose the bravest of those who had been slain. They escorted these warriors to Valhalla, Odin's great hall. The Valkyries are also Odin's messengers. When they go forth on his errands, their armor causes the strange flickering light known as the aurora borealis, the northern lights.

Valkyries are also seen as the angel of death. In addition, they function as cupbearers, offering mead to souls of brave people as they pass over. Valkyries are also guardian spirits who befriend youths, giving them initiatory names and marvelous weapons; they are also regarded as the supernatural bride who teaches the arts of love and war.

Tradition says there are two kinds of Valkyries, the divine and the semi-human, who are only visible to people with second sight. To ordinary people, Valkyries appear as the northern lights.

Valkyries can show you how to face even the toughest of life's challenges with spiritual fortitude, laughter, and joy. They can also show you how to love deeply and passionately. Traditionally, they took brave people to heaven. They also show people how to have courage and what can be accomplished with a little discipline and dedication. They can light up your life with the magic of the northern lights and show you how to float your way to success.

Laima

Associated Culture

Latvian

Laima will help you

- Connect with your holiness and feel whole
- Give birth easily
- Protect your home and yourself
- Call good fortune and good luck into your life
- Embrace your destiny

Invocation

Laima loves song and dance, so sing forth your request. Play your favorite music and allow yourself to dance wildly around the room. Ask for her help from deep within the core of your being. Allow your soul to reach out to her loving presence. She will show you the power of wholeness and holiness.

Laima is the deity of fate. She personifies luck, which can be perceived as good luck or bad. She is the goddess who assists with childbirth. She is honored by women young and old, married or single. Laima controls all the important events in life, such as birth, marriage, and death. She is also the goddess of pregnant women and can ensure a safe and easy pregnancy when she is invited.

Laima is a household goddess of prosperity and good fortune. She is the goddess of new beginnings and is often represented as a beautiful old woman whose face is filled with gentleness and joy. She loves children and helps protect newborns. In some of the older texts, she and her sisters Karta and Dekla represent the trinity of destiny deities. They have the task of influencing the overall destiny of all aspects of human endeavors.

Latvian deities were most often evoked using traditional folk songs and dance. The ancient ones knew that sound had the power to transform and transmute physical matter. Even though Laima works mostly with women, she is more than willing to work with men as well. She knows how hard it is to be in a body incapable of giving birth, in a universe teeming with new beginnings. She would like to help men heal the wounds caused by not having a womb and help them step into the fullness of their being. Not many deities are willing to take on such a deeply healing task.

Sekhmet

Associated Culture

Egyptian

Sekhmet will help you

- Get rid of self-destructive behaviors
- Release any relationships that no longer serve you
- Find a new job
- Create a loving environment

Invocation

Face the west and ask Sekhmet for her assistance.
Light a red candle and allow yourself to hear her wisdom.

Sekhmet's name means "She Who Is Powerful." She is often personified as the aggressive and destructive aspect of the feminine. She is frequently misunderstood and represented in a negative manner. Even though she can be destructive, her actions are never random. She is all-powerful and always tempers her power with the compassion and wisdom of a loving mother. Sekhmet is the patron of physicians, priests, and healers.

Sekhmet is also known as the "eye of Ra." Ra was her father. She is the blinding heat of the noonday sun. Sometimes she is portrayed as a woman with the head of a lioness. Sekhmet is also called "the mistress" and "lady of the tomb," "gracious one," and "destroyer of rebellion." Ra asked her to punish the people who had rebelled against him. She did so with her great power. As soon as the

rebellion was halted, Sekhmet helped the people heal the wounded. She knows much of the ancient wisdom. She is known as the "mighty one of enchantments." Her body is often shown draped in red. She always faces the west.

Sekhmet was worshipped throughout Egypt, but particularly in the area where lions are found. It is said her worship was possibly introduced into Egypt from the Sudan, because lions are more plentiful there. Sekhmet's main center of worship was in Memphis.

Sekhmet will invite you to look at the areas of your life where you sabotage yourself. Where do you rebel against taking those actions that will create exactly what you want? How do you destroy your own happiness? How do you stop yourself from being powerful and speaking your truth?

Ares

Ares will help you

- Absorb hostilities
- Move beyond conflict
- Remember that there are only losers in war
- See the value in choosing love over fear

Invocation

Conflict and strife are very familiar companions. You call upon Ares unconsciously every time you have an argument with someone or judge yourself or someone else. He is the god of war, and chances are you are very good at experiencing conflict. Ares can also help you move beyond senseless suffering created by emotional or physical violence. Ask him to absorb the hostilities and assist you in living in peace instead.

Ares is the Greek god of war or, more accurately, the god of violence. He is a reminder that no one wins in war. When Ares hears the battle cry, he dons his helmet and rushes into battle. In true form, he is unconcerned with who wins or loses as long as massive amounts of blood are shed. As he was always followed by a crowd, they brought with them panic, famine, pain, and oblivion. He was a constant reminder to embrace the higher ideals of love and acceptance and to release all thoughts of anger and judgment.

Ares was distrusted by most of the other gods because he represented heartless action and determination. His sister, Eris, the goddess of discord, and Hades, the god of the dead, sometimes accompanied Ares into battle. Two of Ares's children were Deimos (Fear) and Phobos (Terror). He is a reminder from on high what happens when humans decide to settle disputes with violence rather than find solutions with love.

Ares reminds you that when you focus on the difference, chaos and war ensue. When you acknowledge the similarities and feel the connection, peace is more likely.

Hi'iaka

Associated Culture

Hawaiian

Hi'iaka will help you

- Mend a troublesome relationship
- Feel loved, joyful, and at peace
- Release jealously
- Have a gorgeous garden
- Love yourself unconditionally
- Forgive even the unforgivable

Invocation

Hi'iaka's favorite color is green, so you might want to light a green candle before you ask her for her help. She is very loving and more than willing to help you, so just open your heart and know she will be there for you. She feels most at home under a canopy of trees, so call upon her when you walk in the forest or are planting flowers, trees, or shrubs.

Hi'iaka is Pele's favorite sister. Pele brought her to the island of Hawaii as an egg lovingly carried in her bosom. She is the goddess of Hawaii, of the hills, the lands, the cliffs, and the caves. She is a tender and loving goddess. She especially loves the forest, and she is the daughter of the sea god Kane.

Hi'iaka was entrusted by Pele to go to the island of Kauai to bring back Pele's lover Lohiau. Pele became jealous and killed him with her lava and banished Hi'iaka to the forests, which were protected by her sister Laka, goddess of the forests. Pele also turned her best friend Hopoe into stone. Hopoe still dances on the seashore in Puna. Hi'iaka's lilting laughter can often be heard when you walk under a canopy of trees.

Hi'iaka is a powerful goddess known for her forgiving nature. Her gentleness and joy belie her incredible ability to transform any situation. She knows how to break up stalemates and use nature to heal even the deepest wounds. Hi'iaka knows personally about the destructive nature of jealously and is a wonderful resource when you are dealing with issues of the heart.

Pele

Associated Culture

Hawaiian

Pele will help you

- Increase the passion in your life
- See your life with greater clarity and understanding
- Transform your thinking
- Deal with an unfaithful lover
- Get to the heart of the matter

Invocation

Pele is definitely the goddess of fire. Light a big candle or build a bonfire. Write a letter to this fiery goddess. Tell her what you want to let go of, what you would like to transform, and what you are willing to do. Choose your words carefully. Not only is she a jealous goddess, but she knows how powerful your words are. When the letter feels right, burn it and throw the ashes into the wind. Listen carefully for her guidance and allow her to help you transform your life.

Pele is the fire goddess of the volcano. Her home is on the Big Island of Hawaii. Pele was born in Tahiti, but because of her fiery temper, her father banished her from his islands. She was given a canoe and traveled north in search of a new home. She visited many islands but found something wrong with each one. You can still see the extinct craters she left behind. When she reached the Big Island, she created Kilauea and decided to make it her home. Pele is very happy on Hawaii because it is considered the navel of the world, the place where creation began.

When Pele first arrived in Hawaii, she used her Pa'oa, or digging stick, to strike deep into the earth on Kauai. But then she was attacked by her older sister and left for dead. Pele recovered and fled to Oahu, where she was once again chased away. Finally, she and her sister Na-maka-o-Kahai had a battle to the death on Maui. Pele was torn apart by her sister, and her bones remain as a hill called Ka-iwi-o-Pele.

Upon her death, Pele became a goddess and found a home on Mauna Kea, on the Island of Hawai'i. Pele dug her final fire pit in Halemaumau Crater at the summit of Kilauea. Pele is a powerful and jealous goddess. Her esoteric qualities include physical vitality, psychic awareness, the power of transformation, and the magic and wonder of creation. She is a very powerful goddess and best approached with humility, reverence, and profound admiration.

Osiris

Associated Culture

Egyptian

Osiris will help you

- Utilize your dreams
- Breathe new life into all of your relationships
- Harness the limitless energies of transformation
- Heal your body and your mind

Invocation

Go out on a moonless night and look at the stars. Breathe in the fresh night air and ask for his help. Ask him to guide your thoughts and your actions. He will come to you in your dreams. Pay attention to the symbols and if you are unclear about their meaning, ask him to explain the symbolism to you the following night. He is a patient teacher, especially if you are a willing student.

Osiris ruled the world of man after the god, Ra, left the earth to rule heaven. Men were still cannibals, so Osiris taught them how to farm and brought them civilization. As the god of vegetation, he was also considered the first "green man." A green face that looks like it is made out of overlapping leaves is also a pagan symbol of the guardian of plants and the forest.

Osiris was killed by his brother Seth. His beautiful wife Isis, the sky goddess, was able to magically bring him back to life through her passionate love for him. Because he was the first being to die, he became the god of the underworld. He was worshipped as a fertility god and the god of resurrection. Because he died and was resurrected, he is able to imbue people with the power of transformation and transmutation.

Osiris stands in the hall of truth, able to see both the world of the living and of the dead. He can show you how to reconcile them so you can move beyond the cycle of birth and death. He can teach you to connect with your divine self and, in that process, let go of anything preventing you from feeling the sense of oneness and interdependence the universe is based on.

He knows the great mysteries of the universe. As the god of the dead, Osiris has access to many ancient masters. Osiris is deeply affected by the ability of people to love. He has great compassion for people's needless suffering. His greatest wish is to help people empower themselves so they no longer experience pain and suffering.

Durga

Associated Culture

Hindu

Durga will help you

- Purge all of your personal demons
- Release old trauma and emotional pain
- Let go of any beliefs or situations that no longer serve you

- Fill your life with passion and joy
- Have incredible sex and multiple orgasms

Invocation

Durga likes music and dance, so put on some of your favorite music and dance to it. Sing your request out loudly, with laughter and joy. Playfully ask her for her help. Pink is her favorite color, so you could light a pink candle or twirl around while holding a bright pink scarf.

Durga is the goddess of deliverance and comes to Earth on the seventh day after the new moon in the autumn of each year. She is one of the incarnations of the Mother Goddess, and she will help you get rid of all your personal demons. She is the keeper of the creative energies that keep the cosmos in motion.

Durga is traditionally represented as a ten-armed woman sitting on a lion and wielding many deadly weapons. She was created when demons threatened the existence of the gods and goddesses. To overcome the demons, all the gods sent forth their love and light, and each of them cre-ated a part of Durga's body. In Sanskrit, her name means "invincible" or "unattainable."

Normally, she keeps her awesome creative energy in reserve or channels it as a positive creative force, but when she gets angry, she becomes an alarmingly destruc-tive force. When she is at the side of her lord Shiva, she is calm and peaceful. Her energy is channeled into her Tantric nature, making her a demanding and exuberant sexual partner. Durga will show you how to live life pas-sionately, freely, and with incredible joy and full of bound-less possibilities.

Tate

Associated Culture

Lakota

Tate will help you

- Let go of resistance
- Open up to the limitless possibilities of life
- Experience the magical nature of reality
- Have a good life

Invocation

Go outside and stand where you can feel the wind. Ask Tate to flow through you, filling you with his wisdom, power, and flexibility. When you open up to his fluid nature, your life becomes a magnificent work of art.

In the Lakota myth of creation, Tate, the wind god, is the father of the four winds (North, East, West, and South). Tate was attracted to Ite. Although she wasn't a goddess, she lived at the entrance of the Spirit Trail. After the marriage, Ite had four sons: the North, East, West, and South winds.

The wind that dwells in the west is strong and good. He protects humans from the harmful North wind. Eagles live in the west, and all the animals were created there. The North wind is strong, but cruel. He kills living beings without mercy. The East wind's major role is to bring the dawn with each new day. Okaga, the warm South wind, embraces you. He is the giver of life and is kind to everyone, so you will have a pleasant life. Finally, there is Yumni, the whirlwind, who knows all the games, which are an important part of Dakota society.

Tate is the breath of life. He was born from the motion of creation. He brings blessings to everything he touches. He has the ability to be gentle and loving or destructive. He blows across the earth carrying the seed of the life force with him. Tate can show you how to fill everything in your life with the life-enhancing magic of spirit.

Minerva

Minerva will help you

- Let go of limiting beliefs
- See yourself in a loving and supportive way

- Use your shadow self as a doorway to personal freedom
- Be original and creative

Invocation

Begin by asking yourself what you want to create and then ask Minerva for her help. Place three red roses in a triangle on a pretty piece of cloth, write your request on a small piece of paper, and put it in the center of the triangle. When the roses have wilted, throw away your note. She may ask you a lot of questions, but by exploring them, you will see options you never thought were possible.

Minerva is the Roman goddess of intelligence, creativity, wisdom, medicine, the arts, domestic skills, science and trade, and also of war. Minerva is believed to be the inventor of numbers and musical instruments. Her name comes from the word meaning "mind," so she is the goddess of all workers guided by the mind. She is often depicted with her sacred tree, the olive tree. She wears a headdress with an owl on it because she is also the goddess of death and the great mysteries of the realms of magic.

Minerva asks you to examine your beliefs, find the ones that no longer serve you, and change them. She will help you look at any beliefs or assumptions you have that don't support your holiness. What unhealthy or worn-out beliefs do you hold which stop you from being happy? What self-defeating behaviors do you do regularly? Do other people's opinions of you still matter? Minerva is the goddess of the mind, so she will demand you look at how you use your mind. Does your thinking add to the quality of your life or does it limit your choices?

Life happens, and then you tell yourself a story about what has just happened. Do your stories nurture you or limit you? Minerva will remind you that when you are willing to see your whole self in a loving manner, you will make choices that help you create happiness and joy. She will help you see your shadow self in a new light, one that will set you free.

Acknowledgments

Writing this book has been such an incredible gift. I'd like to thank my wonderful agents, Sheree and Janet, for making it possible and my editor Jill. I had no idea what an incredible adventure this book would be for me. I now have a deep and loving relationship with lots of angels, saints, ascended masters, gods, goddesses, and deities. I'd like to thank them for their willingness and availability.

A special thanks for my supportive family and friends. Without all of them, this book wouldn't have been possible. I'd like to thank Bea for her love, patience, and endless edits. I'd like to thank the world for having angels, magic, and miracles.

And I'd like to thank the world for rainbows.

Author's Note

It has been an incredible honor and privilege to write this book. I anticipate you will enjoy reading this book as much as I enjoyed writing it. I hope you allow yourself to really benefit from all the love and wisdom contained within its pages.

I always love hearing from my readers. If you have any questions or you'd like to contact me, just go to my Web site, susangregg.com.

With lots of love and aloha,
Susan

Glossary

Angel: The term angel comes from the Greek word *angelos*, which means messenger. Angels were created by God to minister to and care for all living beings. They mediate between God and mortals. In the hierarchy of angels, guardian angels are closest to the physical plane.

Archangel: A manager or caretaker of other angels, an archangel has a specialized purpose such as helping human beings feel safe, loved, and nurtured. In some literature, there are only four archangels, while in other belief systems, there are an infinite number.

Ascended master: A being who has become enlightened and serves humanity. Ascended masters have realized they are that divine spark within. They have released all of their limiting beliefs and are able to see all of life through the eyes of love. They can come and go at will from the earth plane and are always willing to be of assistance to anyone who asks.

Ascension: Ascension is a process of letting go of all limiting beliefs and becoming one with the godself. Once that has been accomplished, a person can ascend into heaven or attain nirvana without going through the death process. It is a physical process, as in the ascension of Jesus, as well as an emotional and spiritual process.

Bodhisattva: A person who has become fully enlightened and has attained the necessary perspective to become a Buddha. In Buddhism, there are many Buddhas, although many non-Buddhists are more familiar with Siddhartha Gautama.

Book of Enoch: A book about the sacred knowledge of creation. The Book of Enoch is divided into five basic parts. It was written well before the birth of Jesus, yet the early writings of the Christian Church fathers often refer to it. The book was lost for many centuries and then copies of it were again found in the 1700s.

Book of Raziel: A book of angel magic and mysticism that is said to contain all of the secrets of the universe. It is written in such an ancient language even the angels can't translate it.

Cabala: See *Kabbalah*

Cherubim: In the hierarchy of heaven, cherubim are the second closest to God, and at times they carry his throne. They aren't specifically angels, but they do have wings and have very similar characteristics.

Deity: A god or goddess.

Divinity: A manifestation of the creative god force.

Dominions: The fourth order of angels. They announce God's commands. They are also a channel of mercy and oversee the activities of other angels.

Elemental World: The physical world, specifically anything to do with nature, such as forests, plants, and bodies of water.

Fairies: Supernatural or spiritual beings. They are human in appearance, with wings, and they have special magical powers. They are also referred to as the wee people.

God: The creative energy that manifested the universe. When the word has a small "g," it refers to a personification of that energy of creation.

Goddess: The female aspect of god.

Great White Brotherhood: A spiritual organization composed of those Ascended Masters who have dedicated themselves to helping humanity during this time of great changes.

Heaven: A place where souls go after death. Christianity, Judaism, and Islam each have different ideas about heaven. There are many layers of heaven, often a hierarchy of angels and rulers. It can be an amazingly complex place.

Higher Self: That part of you that is always connected to your spirit. It is the essence of who and what you really are.

Invocation: A way of calling upon or asking for help from a spiritual being. It is often a form of prayer.

Kabbalah: Refers to a body of esoteric or mystic doctrine or teachings concerning God and the nature of the universe. It is said to have been revealed to holy men in the distant past. The knowledge was given only to a select few and was preserved by them over the centuries. The word *Kabbalah* is derived from a Hebrew word meaning "to receive."

Luminaries: In Gnostic writings, they are celestial lights like the sun and the moon. The luminaries are beings, similar to angels, that have special powers.

Order of Principalities: The seventh-highest order of angels. They watch over the action of nations and cities. Each nation and city has its own angel, and they also govern and protect all religions.

Past life: A previous incarnation in physical reality by your soul.

Powers: In the hierarchy of heaven, they are in the sixth order and are entrusted with making sure everything is well ordered and God's orders are precisely carried out.

Reincarnation: A belief in the cycle of life, death, and rebirth. Reincarnation is the ability of the soul to come back in a new body.

Seraphim: The angels closest to God. Their name is thought to be derived from the Hebrew word *saraf*, which means "to burn" and refers to their ability to destroy by means of fire.

Spirit: The energy that gives life to a body, a plant, or any other living being.

Spirit Guides: Spiritual beings that are willing to assist people and guide them. They are much like guardian angels and are more than willing to help you.

Sprite: An elemental, spiritual being who has magical powers. There are water sprites and air sprites. The term *sprite* is also sometimes used to refer to fairies, elves, and dwarfs.

Sumerian Society: Sumer was the world's first civilization. It arose about 3,500 BC in what is now Iraq in the land between the Tigris and the Euphrates.

Thrones: The highest order of angels. The term refers to the majesty of the seat of God.

Virtues: The order of angels that represents maturity and courage. They are entrusted with the movement of all heavenly bodies; therefore, they are also known as heavenly powers.

Index

Note: Locators in italics indicate illustrations.